Ine Van Riet in association with Neil Mc

HORNIMAN'S CHOICE

FOUR ONE ACT PLAYS FROM THE
'MANCHESTER SCHOOL' OF PLAYWRIGHTS

THE PRICE OF COAL by Harold Brighouse

NIGHT WATCHES by Allan Monkhouse

THE OLD TESTAMENT AND THE NEW by Stanley Houghton

LONESOME LIKE by Harold Brighouse

FINBOROUGH | THEATRE

The Price of Coal was first performed at the Scottish Repertory Theatre, Glasgow
on Monday, 15 November 1909.

Lonesome Like was first performed at the Royalty Theatre, Glasgow
on Monday, 6 February 1911.

The Old Testament and the New was first performed at the Gaiety Theatre, Manchester
on Monday, 22 June 1914.

Horniman's Choice was first performed at the Finborough Theatre:
Sunday, 27 September 2015

HORNIMAN'S CHOICE

The Price of Coal by Harold Brighouse

Mary Bradshaw	**Hannah Edwards**
Jack Tyldesley	**Lewis Maiella**
Ellen Tyldesley	**Ursula Mohan**
Polly Livesey	**Jemma Churchill**

The action takes place in Ellen Tyldesley's home, Lancashire, 1909.

Night Watches by Allan Monkhouse

Nurse	**Jemma Churchill**
Orderly	**James Holmes**
First Soldier	**Graham O'Mara**
Second Soldier	**Lewis Maiella**

The action takes place in a Red Cross hospital, 1916.

The Old Testament and the New by Stanley Houghton

Martha Battersby	**Jemma Churchill**
Christopher Battersby	**James Holmes**
Edward Fielding	**Graham O'Mara**
Mary Battersby	**Hannah Edwards**

The action takes place in Danesbridge, South Cheshire, 1914.

Lonesome Like by Harold Brighouse

Sarah Ormerod	**Ursula Mohan**
Emma Brierley	**Hannah Edwards**
Sam Horrocks	**Lewis Maiella**
Reverend Frank Alleyne	**Graham O'Mara**

The action takes place in Sarah Ormerod's home, Lancashire, 1911.

The performance lasts approximately two hours.

There will be one interval of twenty minutes.

Director	**Anna Marsland**
Designer	**Amelia Jane Hankin**
Lighting	**Rob Mills**
Sound	**Simon Gethin Thomas**
Producer	**Ine Van Riet**
Stage Manager	**Joy Laing**
Costume Supervisor	**Lesley McKirdy**

Jemma Churchill | Polly Livesey, Nurse and Martha Battersby

Trained at Guildhall School of Music and Drama.
Theatre includes *My Name is Freda*, *Unearthed*, *Larksong*, *The Gift* (New Vic Theatre, Newcastle-under-Lyme), *84 Charing Cross Road* (Salisbury Playhouse), *Hungry* (National Tour), *Factors Unseen* (Orange Tree Theatre, Richmond), *Slaughterhouse Five* (Everyman Theatre, Liverpool), *Macbeth* (London Bubble), *Hamlet* (Theatre Museum), *Breaking The Code* (English Theatre, Frankfurt), *Noises Off* (New Wolsey Theatre, Ipswich), *The Good Mother* (Landor Theatre), *Little Pieces of Gold* (Theatre503), *A Night in Provence* (The Mill at Sonning), *The Notebook of Trigorin* (Northcott Theatre, Exeter), *I'll Be Back Before Midnight* (Theatre By the Lake, Keswick), *The Boys From Hibernia* (Belgrade Theatre, Coventry) and *The Last Waltz* (Gateway Theatre, Chester).
Film includes *Deny Everything*, *Between Places*, *Burn The Clock*, *Beached* and *Desert Flower*.
Television includes *Agatha Raisin and the Quiche of Death*, *Upstairs Downstairs*, *Waterloo Road*, *The Liquid Bomb Plot*, *Hollyoaks*, *Doctors*, *Jekyll*, *Heartbeat*, *Holby City*, *Living It*, *Murder in Suburbia*, *Footballer's Wives*, *Crossroads*, *Midsomer Murders*, *Murder in Mind*, *Where There's Smoke*, *Kiss Me Kate*, *Red Dwarf*, *Dangerfield*, *Jonathan Creek*, *EastEnders* and *Waiting for God*.
Radio includes *Sherlock Holmes*, *Doctor Who*, *Blakes 7*, *Brief Lives*, *The Good Companions* and *Potting On*.

Hannah Edwards | Mary Bradshaw, Mary Battersby and Emma Brierley

Trained at Bristol Old Vic Theatre School.
Theatre includes *She Stoops to Conquer* (Northern Broadsides), *Inherit the Wind*, *I Don't Want to Set the World on Fire*, *101 Dalmatians*, *A Christmas Carol*, *Alice in Wonderland* (New Vic Theatre, Newcastle-under-Lyme), *Romeo and Juliet* (Theatre Royal Bury St Edmunds), *Country Music* (Trafalgar Studios), *Rumpole of the Bailey* (Bath Literary Festival) and *Chitty Chitty Bang Bang* (London Palladium).
Film includes *Alternative Voting* and *Flowers*.
Television includes *Call the Midwife*, *Being April*, *Life Begins* and *The Priory*.
Radio includes *The Chess Girls* and *Charley From Outside*.

James Holmes | Orderly and Christopher Battersby

Trained at The Poor School.
Theatre includes *Aladdin* (Buxton Opera House), *Romeo and Juliet*, *The Wind in the Willows*, *The Merry Wives of Windsor* (Grosvenor Park Open Air Theatre), *Portia Coughlin*, *The List*, *Dear Aunty Elvis* (Old Red Lion Theatre), *Making Stalin Laugh* (JW3 Theatre), *@War*, *Who's Afraid of the Big Bad Wolf?*, *Present Tense: The Beginning*, *Present Tense: Just*

Us (Southwark Playhouse), *Potholes*, *Talking in Bed* (Theatre503), *Rain Man* (English Theatre, Frankfurt), *The Lady in the Van*, *The Flint Street Nativity*, *Happy Now* (Hull Truck Theatre), *The Dumb Waiter* (Guildhall Theatre, Derby), *Relax* (Warehouse Theatre, Croydon), *Ignition: Paper Kite* (Tristan Bates Theatre), *The Country Wife* (Bridewell Theatre), *Measure for Measure*, *The Importance of Being Earnest* (New Players Theatre), *Twelfth Night* (Ripley Castle Open Air Theatre) and the original production of *Anorak of Fire* (Edinburgh Festival, Arts Theatre and National Tour).
Film includes *Lava*.
Television includes *I Live With Models*, *Phoneshop*, *The Javone Prince Show*, *Miranda*, *Dani's House*, *Psychoville*, *How TV Ruined Your Life*, *Unwrapped with Miranda Hart*, *The Last Enemy*, *Love Soup*, *Big Brother's Bit On The Side*, *Coronation Street*, *Harry Hill's TV Burp*, *My Boy Jack*, *Gayle Tuesday - The Comeback*, *Doctors*, *The Bill*, *Two Pints of Lager and a Packet of Crisps*, *Coked Up Britain*, *Open Wide*, *Peep Show*, *Jane Hall*, *The Catherine Tate Show*, *Spooks*, *My Hero*, *Rhona*, *Stop The World* and *The Office*.
Radio includes *Spike's Lookalikes*, *Peacefully in their Sleeps* and *Agatha Raisin*.

Lewis Maiella | Jack Tyldesley, Second Soldier and Sam Horrocks

Trained at Arts Educational Schools London.
Theatre includes *1984*, *The Last Days of Judas Iscariot*, *King Lear*, *A View from the Bridge* and *You Can Still Make A Killing* (Arts Educational Schools London).
Film includes *The Morning After*.

Ursula Mohan | Ellen Tyldesley and Sarah Ormerod

Productions at the Finborough Theatre include *Outward Bound*, *Eyes Catch Fire*, *Trelawny Of The Wells*, *The Lower Depths* and *Online And Paranoid in the Sentimental City*.
Trained at Webber Douglas.
Theatre includes *The Veil (National Theatre)*, *Women of Troy*, *Blood Wedding* (The Steam Industry at the Scoop), *King Lear* (Union Theatre), *Elegies* (Criterion Theatre), *Dad's Army Marches On* (UK Tour), *The Drowsy Chaperone* (Upstairs at the Gatehouse), *The Winter's Tale* (Courtyard Theatre), *Ala In Tango* and Peter Brook's *US* (Royal Shakespeare Company), *Making Tracks* (Stephen Joseph Theatre, Scarborough), *Bevan* (Sherman Cymru, Cardiff), *Antigone* (Greenwich Theatre), *The Good Woman Of Setzuan* (Hampstead Theatre), *A Murder Is Announced* (Vaudeville Theatre), *Revenge* (Royal Court Theatre), *Othello* (Open Air Theatre, Regent's Park), *The Cenci* (Almeida Theatre), *Bloody Mary* (Theatre Royal Stratford East) and *Scapino* (The Young Vic).
Film includes *The Bank Job* and *Friends Pictured Within*.
Television includes *Holby City* and *On The Buses*.

Graham O'Mara | First Soldier, Edward Fielding and Reverend Frank Alleyne

Productions at the Finborough Theatre include *Hindle Wakes*. Theatre includes *Romeo and Juliet*, *The Merry Wives of Windsor*, *Wind in the Willows*, *A Midsummer Night's Dream, Othello* (Grosvenor Park Open Air Theatre), *Sense and Sensibility* (Watermill Theatre, Newbury), *Cans* (Theatre503), *Alice* (Crucible Theatre, Sheffield), *Pedal Pusher*, *The Winter's Tale* (Theatre Delicatessen), *FOOD* (Traverse Theatre, Edinburgh, National Tour and BAC), *David Copperfield* (National Tour), *Sweet Love Remembered*, *Hamlet* (Shakespeare's Globe), *Bumps*, *Brother My Brother* (Warehouse Theatre, Croydon), *Born Angry* (Etcetera Theatre), *A Man of Letters* (Orange Tree Theatre, Richmond), *The Government Inspector*, *The Three Musketeers* (The Young Vic), *Romeo and Juliet* (Wild Thyme), *The Rise and Fall of Little Voice* (Theatre Royal Bury St Edmunds) and *Emma* (National Tour).
Television includes *Friday Night Dinner*, *The Queen*, *Waterloo Road*, *Casualty* and *Silent Witness*.

Harold Brighouse | Playwright, *The Price of Coal* and *Lonesome Like*

Playwright Harold Brighouse (1882–1958) remains best known for his 1916 classic *Hobson's Choice*. The story of how a tyrannical Lancashire boot maker is brought down to earth by his daughter and her simple husband, *Hobson's Choice* has been much revived and was last seen in London at The Young Vic in 2003. It was filmed by David Lean with Charles Laughton and John Mills, and even adapted into a ballet. Brighouse brought a new and groundbreaking style to British theatre, portraying the bleak and harsh lives of the working classes, but combining it with a unique Northern flavour and wit. The Finborough Theatre revived Harold Brighouse's *The Northerners* in 2010.

Stanley Houghton | Playwright, *The Old Testament and the New*

Stanley Houghton (1881 – 1913) was born in Ashton-upon-Mersey, Sale, Cheshire. Educated at Manchester Grammar School, he went into his father's cotton business where he worked until the success of *Hindle Wakes* in 1912 allowed him to finally achieve his ambition to become a professional writer. He died just a year later of meningitis. Houghton's other works include *The Intrigues*, *The Reckoning*, *The Dear Departed*, *Independent Means* (recently revived by the Library Theatre, Manchester), *The Younger Generation*, *The Master of the House*, *Fancy-Free*, *Trust the People* and *The Perfect Cure*. The Finborough Theatre presented an acclaimed revival of *Hindle Wakes* in 2012 to mark the centenary of its world premiere.

Allan Monkhouse | Playwright, *Night Watches*

Allan Monkhouse (1858 – 1936) was an English playwright, critic, essayist and novelist. He was born in Barnard Castle, County Durham. He worked in the cotton trade, in Manchester, and settled in Disley, Cheshire. From 1902 to 1932 he worked on *The Manchester Guardian*, writing also for *The New Statesman*. He began to write drama for the Gaiety Theatre, Manchester, shortly after it was opened by Annie Horniman. His best known plays include *Mary Broome* and *The Conquering Hero*, both recently revived by the Orange Tree Theatre, Richmond.

Anna Marsland | Director

Productions at the Finborough Theatre include directing the staged reading of *One For All* as part of *Vibrant 2014 – A Festival of Finborough Playwrights*.
Trained on the MFA Theatre Directing course at Birkbeck College, and was a finalist for the 2013 JMK Award for Young Directors.
Theatre includes *Twelfth Night* (Victoria Baths, Manchester), *Masterclass Academy Showcase* (Theatre Royal Haymarket), *The Leonardo Question* (Rosemary Branch Theatre and Roxy Art House), *Secret Heart*, *Road*, *All the Ordinary Angels*, *What the Butler Saw* and *Two* (ADC Theatre).
Assistant Direction includes *The White Devil*, *The Roaring Girl* (Royal Shakespeare Company), *Hope Light and Nowhere* (Underbelly Theatre, Edinburgh), *A Christmas Carol* (New Vic Theatre, Newcastle-under-Lyme), *Lady Windermere's Fan*, *Miss Julie*, *The Gatekeeper*, *Beautiful Thing* and *Good* (Royal Exchange Theatre, Manchester), *Othello* (Rose Theatre, Bankside, and Broadway Theatre, Barking) and *Love and Money* (Arts Educational Schools).
As Text Assistant, theatre includes *The Malcontent* (Sam Wanamaker Playhouse) and *Henry VI: Parts I, II, and III* (Shakespeare's Globe).
She is currently Resident Director on the National Theatre's production of *The Curious Incident of the Dog in the Night-Time* in the West End.

Amelia Jane Hankin | Designer

Trained at the Royal Academy of Dramatic Art.
Theatre includes *The Nightmare Before Christmas* (West Yorkshire Playhouse), *Fake It 'Til You Make It* (National Tour, Traverse Theatre, Edinburgh, and Soho Theatre), *64 Squares* (National Tour and Edinburgh Festival), *Unearthed* (National Tour and Arcola Theatre), *Mother Courage and her Children* (Drama Centre, London), *The Itinerant Music Hall* (Lyric Theatre, Hammersmith, and Watford Palace Theatre), *The Box* (Theatre Delicatessen), *You Once Said Yes* (The Roundhouse, The Lowry, Salford, Nuffield Theatre, Southampton, and Perth International Festival, Australia), *The Red Helicopter* (Arcola Theatre), *The Many Whoops of Whoops Town* (Lyric Theatre, Hammersmith) and *Cinderella* (Charing Cross Theatre).
Associate and Assistant Designs include *A Midsummer Night's Dream*, *Death of a Salesman*, *The Christmas Truce* (Royal Shakespeare Company) and *Pests* (Royal Court Theatre and Royal Exchange Theatre, Manchester).

Rob Mills | Lighting Designer

Productions at the Finborough include *I Wish to Die Singing*, *Obama-ology*, *Free as Air, Sommer 14* and *Gay's the Word*.

Theatre includes *Love Birds* (Edinburgh Festival), *Crows on the Wire* (Northern Ireland Tour), *Romeo and Juliet* (Cambridge Arts Theatre), *Oedipus Retold, Making Dickie Happy* (Tristan Bates Theatre), *Tosca* (National Tour and Luxembourg National Cultural Centre), *Salad Days*, *Biograph Girl*, *Daredevas* (Waterman's Theatre), *Gilbert is Dead* (Hoxton Hall), *Love Bites* (Leatherhead Theatre), *The Elixir of Love* (Stanley Hall Opera), *Napoleon Noir* (Shaw Theatre), *The Lion the Witch and the Wardrobe, Hayton on Homicide* (Edinburgh), *Niceties* (Cambridge Footlights), *Aida* (Epsom Playhouse), *Madama Butterfly* (Harlequin Theatre), *Venus and Adonis*, *Dido and Aeneas*, *The Magic Flute* (Upstairs at the Gatehouse), *The Mikado*, *The Girl and Yeomen of the Guard* (Minack Theatre), *Don Giovanni*, *Pelléas et Mélisande* (West Road Concert Hall) and *Crave* (Edinburgh Festival).

Rob has also provided the lighting & event design for a large number of live and corporate events (which he does as his company Light Motif), ranging from the 2010 'Floating Finale' to the Lord Mayor's Show, on the River Thames, and the 2015 BAFTA TV Awards After Party.

Simon Gethin Thomas | Sound Designer

Trained at Royal Welsh College of Music and Drama. Sound Designs include *Harry the King* (Edinburgh Festival), *Othello Deconstructed* (North Wall Theatre, Oxford), *Ham* (The Space), *I, Cinna* (St James Theatre Studio), *Macbeth* (Cambridge American Stage Tour), *The Seagull*, *The House of Bernarda Alba*, *The Hothouse* and *All the Ordinary Angels* (ADC Theatre). Lighting Designs includes *Eventide* (Arcola Theatre), *Rhythm of Silence* (The Egg, Bath Theatre Royal), *Visitors* (Bush Theatre), *Eye of a Needle* (Southwark Playhouse), *Sweeney Todd* (Twickenham Theatre), *Pincher Martin* (Britten Theatre), *Gone Viral*, *I, Cinna* (St James Theatre), *Girl From Nowhere*, *Woman in the Dunes* (Theatre503), *Fear of Music* (National Tour) and for the Arensky Chamber Orchestra (Queen Elizabeth Hall, Southbank Centre).

Ine Van Riet | Producer

Trained on the MA Creative Producing course at Birkbeck College. She is currently the General Manager at Iris Theatre and Development Officer at the Bush Theatre. She was previously Associate Producer and Development Officer at Tara Arts. Theatre includes *Twelfth Night*, *Pinocchio* (Iris Theatre), *Eye of a Needle* (Southwark Playhouse), *Mucky Kid* (Theatre503), *Sita's Story* (National Tour), *Harlesden High Street* (Tara Arts), *Museum of Broken Relationships* and *Equal Writes* (Tristan Bates Theatre).

Joy Laing | Stage Manager

Trained at London Academy of Music and Dramatic Art.

Theatre includes *A Midsummer Night's Dream in New Orleans* (Arts Theatre), *Il Trittico* (Opera Holland Park), *The Ring Cycle Plays* (Gods and Monsters Theatre at The Scoop), The *Low Road*, *Love, Love, Love*, *Rent*, *Love's Labours Lost*, *The English Game* and *Attempts On Her Life* (London Academy of Music and Dramatic Art).

Lesley McKirdy | Costume
Supervisor

Trained at the Royal Academy of
Dramatic Art.
Theatre includes *La Boheme,
The Wild Man of the West Indies*,
Andromache (Hackney Empire),
*Sweet Charity, The Merry Wives of
Windsor, She Stoops to Conquer,
The Witch of Edmonton, The
Daughter-in-Law* and *In the
Summer House* (Royal Academy of
Dramatic Art).

Production Acknowledgements
We would like to thank Royal College of Music, Iris Theatre, Royal Academy
of Dramatic Arts, National Theatre, Matt Jones, Siu-See Hung, Sophia
Sibthorpe, Mary Marsland, The Young Vic and London Academy of Music
and Dramatic Art.

FINBOROUGH | THEATRE

VIBRANT NEW WRITING | UNIQUE REDISCOVERIES

118 Finborough Road, London SW10 9ED

admin@finboroughtheatre.co.uk | www.finboroughtheatre.co.uk

"A disproportionately valuable component of the London theatre ecology. Its programme combines new writing and revivals, in selections intelligent and audacious."
Financial Times

"The tiny but mighty Finborough… one of the best batting averages of any London company."
Ben Brantley, *The New York Times*

"The Finborough Theatre, under the artistic direction of Neil McPherson, has been earning a place on the must-visit list with its eclectic, smartly curated slate of new works and neglected masterpieces."
Vogue

Founded in 1980, the multi-award-winning Finborough Theatre presents plays and music theatre, concentrated exclusively on vibrant new writing and unique rediscoveries from the 19th and 20th centuries. Our programme is unique – never presenting work that has been seen anywhere in London during the last 25 years. Behind the scenes, we continue to discover and develop a new generation of theatre makers – through our Literary team, and our programmes for both interns and Resident Assistant Directors.

Despite remaining completely unsubsidised, the Finborough Theatre has an unparalleled track record of attracting the finest talent who go on to become leading voices in British theatre. Under Artistic Director Neil McPherson, it has discovered some of the UK's most exciting new playwrights including Laura Wade, James Graham, Mike Bartlett, Jack Thorne, Simon Vinnicombe, Alexandra Wood, Nicholas de Jongh and Anders Lustgarten; and directors including Blanche McIntyre, Robert Hastie and Sam Yates.

Artists working at the theatre in the 1980s included Clive Barker, Rory Bremner, Nica Burns, Kathy Burke, Ken Campbell, Jane Horrocks and Claire Dowie. In the 1990s, the Finborough Theatre first became known for new writing including Naomi Wallace's first play *The War Boys*; Rachel Weisz in David Farr's *Neville Southall's Washbag*; four plays by Anthony Neilson including *Penetrator* and *The Censor*, both of which transferred to the Royal Court Theatre; and new plays by Richard Bean, Lucinda Coxon, David Eldridge, Tony Marchant and Mark Ravenhill. New writing development included the premieres of modern classics such as Mark Ravenhill's *Shopping and F***ing*, Conor McPherson's *This Lime Tree Bower*, Naomi Wallace's *Slaughter City* and Martin McDonagh's *The Pillowman*.

Since 2000, new British plays have included Laura Wade's London debut *Young Emma*, commissioned for the Finborough Theatre; two one-woman shows by Miranda Hart; James Graham's *Albert's Boy* with Victor Spinetti; Sarah Grochala's *S27*; Peter Nichols' *Lingua Franca*, which transferred Off-Broadway; Dawn King's *Foxfinder*; and West End transfers for Joy Wilkinson's *Fair*; Nicholas de Jongh's *Plague Over England*; and Jack Thorne's *Fanny and Faggot*. The late Miriam Karlin made her last stage appearance in *Many Roads to Paradise* in 2008.

We have also produced our annual festival of new writing – *Vibrant – A Festival of Finborough Playwrights* annually since 2009.

UK premieres of foreign plays have included plays by Brad Fraser, Lanford Wilson, Larry Kramer, Tennessee Williams, the English premiere of Robert McLellan's Scots language classic, *Jamie the Saxt*; and three West End transfers – Frank McGuinness' *Gates of Gold* with William Gaunt and John Bennett; Joe DiPietro's *F***ing Men*; and Craig Higginson's *Dream of the Dog* with Dame Janet Suzman.

Rediscoveries of neglected work – most commissioned by the Finborough Theatre – have included the first London revivals of Rolf Hochhuth's *Soldiers* and *The Representative*; both parts of Keith Dewhurst's *Lark Rise to Candleford*; *The Women's War*, an evening of original suffragette plays; *Etta Jenks* with Clarke Peters and Daniela Nardini; Noël Coward's first play, *The Rat Trap*; Charles Wood's *Jingo* with Susannah Harker; Emlyn Williams' *Accolade*; Lennox Robinson's *Drama at Inish* with Celia Imrie and Paul O'Grady; John Van Druten's *London Wall* which transferred to St James' Theatre; and J. B. Priestley's *Cornelius* which transferred to a sell out Off Broadway run in New York City.

Music Theatre has included the new (premieres from Grant Olding, Charles Miller, Michael John LaChuisa, Adam Guettel, Andrew Lippa, Paul Scott Goodman, and Adam Gwon's *Ordinary Days* which transferred to the West End) and the old (the UK premiere of Rodgers and Hammerstein's *State Fair* which also transferred to the West End), and the acclaimed 'Celebrating British Music Theatre' series.

The Finborough Theatre won *The Stage* Fringe Theatre of the Year Award in 2011, *London Theatre Reviews'* Empty Space Peter Brook Award in 2010 and 2012, the Empty Space Peter Brook Award's Dan Crawford Pub Theatre Award in 2005 and 2008, the Empty Space Peter Brook Mark Marvin Award in 2004, and swept the board with eight awards at the 2012 OffWestEnd Awards including Best Artistic Director and Best Director for the second year running. *Accolade* was named Best Fringe Show of 2011 by *Time Out*. It is the only unsubsidised theatre ever to be awarded the Channel 4 Playwrights Scheme nine times.

www.finboroughtheatre.co.uk

The Finborough Theatre is a member of the Independent Theatre Council, the Society of Independent Theatres, Musical Theatre Network, The Friends of Brompton Cemetery and The Earl's Court Society www.earlscourtsociety.org.uk

Supported by

Follow Us Online

 www.facebook.com/FinboroughTheatre

 www.twitter.com/finborough

Mailing

Email admin@finboroughtheatre.co.uk or give your details to our Box Office staff to join our free email list. If you would like to be sent a free season leaflet every three months, just include your postal address and postcode.

Feedback

We welcome your comments, complaints and suggestions. Write to Finborough Theatre, 118 Finborough Road, London SW10 9ED or email us at admin@finboroughtheatre.co.uk

Playscripts

Many of the Finborough Theatre's plays have been published and are on sale from our website.

Finborough Theatre T Shirts

Finborough Theatre T Shirts are on sale from the Box Office, available in Small and Medium £7.00.

Friends

The Finborough Theatre is a registered charity. We receive no public funding, and rely solely on the support of our audiences. Please do consider supporting us by becoming a member of our Friends of the Finborough Theatre scheme. There are various categories of Friends, each offering a wide range of benefits.

Richard Tauber Friends – Val Bond. James Brown. Tom Erhardt. Stephen and Jennifer Harper. Bill Hornby. Richard Jackson. Mike Lewendon. John Lawson. Harry MacAuslan. Mark and Susan Nichols. Sarah Thomas. Kathryn McDowall. Barry Serjent. Stephen Winningham.

Lionel Monckton Friends – Philip G Hooker. Martin and Wendy Kramer. Deborah Milner. Maxine and Eric Reynolds.

William Terriss Friends – Stuart Ffoulkes. Leo and Janet Liebster. Paul and Lindsay Kennedy. Corinne Rooney. Jon and NoraLee Sedmak.

HORNIMAN'S CHOICE

HORNIMAN'S CHOICE

FOUR ONE ACT PLAYS FROM THE 'MANCHESTER SCHOOL' OF PLAYWRIGHTS

THE PRICE OF COAL
by Harold Brighouse

NIGHT WATCHES
by Allan Monkhouse

THE OLD TESTAMENT AND THE NEW
by Stanley Houghton

LONESOME LIKE
by Harold Brighouse

OBERON BOOKS
LONDON

WWW.OBERONBOOKS.COM

This collection first published in 2015 by Oberon Books Ltd
521 Caledonian Road, London N7 9RH
Tel: +44 (0) 20 7607 3637 / Fax: +44 (0) 20 7607 3629
e-mail: info@oberonbooks.com
www.oberonbooks.com

A catalogue record for this book is available from the British
Library.

PB ISBN: 9781783192915
E ISBN: 9781783192922

Printed, bound and converted
by CPI Group (UK) Ltd, Croydon, CR0 4YY.

Visit www.oberonbooks.com to read more about all our books
and to buy them. You will also find features, author interviews and
news of any author events, and you can sign up for e-newsletters
so that you're always first to hear about our new releases.

Contents

THE PRICE OF COAL
BY HAROLD BRIGHOUSE

Modern industrialism has evolved its special types, and the Lancashire collier is small and wiry. He swings a pickaxe for hours on end crouched in an impossibly small space in a heated atmosphere, and physique on the grand scale is unsuited to such conditions. He takes tremendous risks as part of his daily routine. His recreations are, to a fastidious taste, coarse. He works hard under ground, and plays hard above ground. Constrained attitude is so much his second nature that he sits in perfect comfort on his haunches, in the pictured pose of the mild Hindu, his back to a wall, discussing, amongst expectoration – a long row of him – football, dogs, his last spree and his next, the police reports, women.

Altogether a most unpleasant person, this undersized, foul-mouthed, sporting hewer of coal – until you come to know him better, to discover his simplicity of soul, his directness, his matter-of-fact self-sacrifice, the unconscious heroism of his life: and to lose sight of his superficial frailties in your admiration for his finer qualities.

The womenkind of the colliers are marked by the life of the pits no less than the men. They are rough, capable housewives, dressing with more care for durability than effect, tolerant of their menfolk's weaknesses, and, above all stamped with the pit-side stoicism apt to be mistaken for callousness. The sudden death of their breadwinner is an everyday hazard, accepted without complaint and without concealment as part of their life. Like their husbands, they exist from hand to mouth on the brink of eternity. Thrift, when any day's work may be your last, seems a misplaced virtue. Lean fare approaches as payday recedes, and illness, meagrely provided for by membership of a "sick" society, is tided over in the main by the unfailing generosity of neighbours whose own tables suffer by the charity.

The Scene represents the living room of a collier's cottage in Lancashire. The room has three doors, R, L, and C; that at the C. leading out, the R. to the stairs and the L. to a bedroom on the ground floor. The fireplace is R, and the window at the back with the holland blind drawn. The room contains a table (plain deal), chairs, and a comfortable rocking chair placed by the fireplace. There is a dresser with cupboards in its lower portion and a plate-rack over it L. A bird cage hands in the window. Small clock, tea canister, etc., on the mantelpiece.

As the curtain rises the room is in darkness, the time being 5.30am. MARY BRADSHAW, a girl of about twenty, enters from the door R., goes to the gas bracket which hangs over the table, strikes a match on the box she holds in her hand and lights the gas, which has no globe. The girl is just up and not at her best. Her dark hair has been hurriedly screwed up; she has list slippers and a drab skirt. After lighting the gas she finishes fastening her print blouse, which buttons at the front. There is a small spirit-lamp on the hob, with a little tin kettle on it. She lights the lamp. Then she goes to the door L. and knocks upon it.

MARY: Art oop, Jack? It's gone ha'f-past five.

JACK: *(Within)* All reeght. A'll be there in a minute.

MARY takes a plain apron from a hook over the dresser and puts it on briskly, then takes a cup and saucer from the rack, putting them on the dresser, from the cupboard of which she takes a cocoa-tin and puts a spoonful of cocoa in the the cup. Then she takes bread and meat from the cupboard and makes one or two huge rough sandwiches. These she puts on a plate, covers with another plate, and ties in a large red handkerchief with the ends looped for carrying. A tin can with a screw top is placed nearby. Enter L. JACK TYLDESLEY, MARY's cousin, a young collier. JACK is dressed in his working or "black" clothes, which may have been coloured once but are now blackened with coal-dust. He wears no collar, but a muffler which, doffed in the pit, retains some signs of its original red shade. He is lithe and wiry but of no great stature. He carries a miner's safety-lamp in his hand, and places it on the table by the food which MARY has prepared. As he comes, MARY goes to the stove and makes his cocoa.

A weren't hardly looking for to see thee this morning, Mary.

MARY: *(Going on with her operations at the stove.)* Bless the lad, why not? Mebbe yo'd raither A dragged thy moother out o' her bed and her wi' her rheumatics an' all.

JACK: A'd 'ave done for masel' for once in a way.

MARY: Nice mess tha'd mak' o' the job.

JACK: A'm not a babby.

MARY: A fancy A can see thee doing it an' getting to the pit behind time an' all. We've noan quarrelled, have we?

JACK: Not as A knows on.

MARY: Then why shouldn't A get up an' do for yo', same as A have done pretty near as long as A can call to mind?

JACK: A dunno.

MARY: No, nor any one else neither.

JACK: *(Apologetically.)* Fact is A thowt mebbe after what we was saying last neeght as yo'd noan care to see me this morning.

MARY: Nay, there's nowt upsettin' in that as A sees to mak' me seek owt other than what's usual.

JACK: *(Bending over her – eagerly.)* Then, wilt thou tell me –

MARY: *(Cutting him short and putting the cocoa on the table – dryly.)* There's thy cocoa. Best drink it while it's hot.

JACK: Aye.

(He takes a sup and puts the cup down quickly, spluttering.)

It is hot, an' all.

MARY: It's a cold morning to turn out into. Yo'll do wi' summat hot this weather.

JACK: Aye. A dessay 'tis, but weather can wait. A've summat else to talk about to thee besides weather.

MARY: Mebbe tha hast, my lad, an' mebbe tha'll talk about it when proper time cooms.

JACK: *(Pleadingly.)* Mary, lass, must A wait until to-neeght for an answer?

MARY: *(Drawing back.)* Play fair now, Jack. Yo' give a day from last neeght to think on it.

JACK: A know A did. That's reeght enough. Only waiting's not so blamed easy as A thowt when it cooms to doing it.

MARY: Happen it's not. But tha'll have to put up wi' it. Waiting were thy notion. A didn't ask for it.

JACK: *(Appealingly.)* Don't be hard on a chap, Mary. A want thee that bad, lass, A'm on pricks till A know which road cat's going to jump. Tha never knows what's a-going to chance down pit. Think, lass. A might never coom up again and th'd be sick an' sorry if A were blowed to kingdom come wi'out the consolation o' knowing tha meant to have me.

MARY: No, tha don't, my lad. Tha'll not frighten me that road. A'm noan pit-born like yo', but A've lived alongside pits too long for that. And tha knows very well it's noan reeght to talk about them things. A towld thee A'd give thee thy answer to-neeght an' tha'll bide till to-neeght for it. A'm noan going back on my word.

JACK: But if tha knows what tha's going to say why can't tha tell me now and put me out o' my misery?

MARY: Aye, an' have thee going round telling folks tha'd nobbut to whistle an' A rushed into thy arms. No, my lad, A'm a single woman yet an' A'm noan promised to any man. A'll tak' my own time to tell thee whether A'm game to change my name or not.

(Breaking off and looking at clock.) It's time tha was flitting. Tha'll be late if tha doan't get a move on.

JACK: *(Sullenly.)* A doan't care if A am.

MARY: Yes, tha dost. Tha's no need to turn stupid. Tha's noan missed being in first cage down sin' tha's bin going to pit, an' A'll noan have it said tha started missing it through me. Hast finished tha cocoa?

JACK: *(Drinking it up.)* Aye. Tha's rare an' hard on a chap, Mary.

MARY: Get along wi' thee. If tha'd bin as hot on for weddin'
me as tha reckons thasel', mebbe tha'd have upped an'
asked me a bit sooner.

JACK: *(Protestingly.)* A nobbut waited while my mind were
mad' oop proper. A asked thee sharp enough when it were.

MARY: Then tha'll wait while mine's made oop. What's sauce
for th' goose is sauce for th' gander.

JACK: Yo' couldn't give me so much as an 'int now? Nobbut a
lick an' a promise like?

MARY: Nay, A'm makking no promises till A'm ready. Tha's
only wasting thy time and chancing being late, an' all.

JACK: *(Resignedly.)* Eh well, if A mun wait, A mun wait.

MARY: Evening 'ull coom before tha knows it.

JACK: *(Going to door L. and taking his cap from a peg on the door.)*
Oh aye. Talking's easy. Yo're nobbut having me on a piece
o' string all time, teasing wench. It's mebbe fun to thee, but
it's no ways fun to me carrying on wilful like that. *(Putting
his cap on.)*

MARY: *(Threateningly.)* Tha'll mak' thyself late for thy work.
That's what's going to be th' end of it.

JACK: All reeght. A'm going. Where's my baggin'?

*MARY hands the handkerchief of food and the can, which he slings
over his shoulder by a short strap attached to it.*

MARY: There tha art.

JACK: Hast wrapped 'un oop well?

MARY: Aye. Why?

JACK: Rats was busy at 'un yesterday when A coom to put my
pick down an' feel for my dinner. But yo' canna help rats
in a pit, an' happen they're as hungry as A am.

MARY: Well, it's made up as fast as A can get it. *(Looking at clock.)* Now look sharp or tha'll be late.

JACK turns to go.

Tha's forgetting thy lamp. Wheerever would'st be if A weren't oop to look after thee?

JACK: It's wi' thinking of thee, lass. *(Taking the lamp.)*

MARY: Time enough for that when thy shift's over.

JACK: *(At the door C.)* A'll be whoam pretty sharp when it is, so tha'd best be ready.

MARY: A'll be ready reeght enough.

JACK: All reeght. Then we'll leave it at that.

MARY: Aye.

Exit JACK.

MARY holds the door open and stands for a moment watching him go. He turns in the direction remote from the window. Morning is breaking, and the first grey light is visible through the door. She closes it and then draws the blind up: as she does so ELLEN TYLDESLEY, JACK's mother enters, through the door R. She is an old woman, spare in figure, and bearing the signs of a hard life. She is dressed plainly in black. MARY starts round in surprise from the blind as the door opens.

(Going towards her.) Why, aunt, you're up early.

ELLEN: *(Standing by the door.)* Aye. Has the lad gone?

MARY: He's nobbut just gone out. Is anything the matter?

ELLEN: No, lass, no. A'd a fancy to see him afore he went, that's all.

MARY: Shall A run after him? He's only just this minute gone.

ELLEN: An' mak' him late? No, we munna do that. It were nobbut a fancy. A thowt A might catch him, but A'll noan chance makking him late. He tak's a pride in being there reg'lar for first cage down, an' he'd be rare an' mad wi' me if A called 'un back for nowt.

MARY: Why didn't yo' shout us from your room?

ELLEN: A didn't think to.

MARY: *(Puzzled but consoling.)* Well A'm sorry tha left thy bed for nothing, before the room's aired too.

ELLEN: That's nowt, lass.

MARY: *(Briskly.)* Well, sit thee down while A mak' fire an' get the breakfast ready. Room 'ull soon be warm.

ELLEN: *(Absently.)* Aye, lass.

ELLEN moves listlessly across and sits passively in the rocking-chair. MARY takes some sticks and paper out of the oven and kneels to make a fire.

MARY: It's a bit sharp this morning, too.

Without turning, she does on with her fire, lighting the sticks and putting on coal. ELLEN does not reply, but puts a handkerchief to her eyes. MARY gets up smartly and turns, seeing ELLEN's distress.

Aunt, what is it? Won't yo' tell me what's troubling you?

ELLEN: Nowt, lass, nowt.

MARY: But there must be summat. What made yo' get oop so early? Yo' were sleeping sound enough when A left you.

ELLEN: Sleeping? Aye, A were sleeping reeght enough, an' would to God A weren't.

MARY: What dost mean?

ELLEN: Only an owd woman's fancy, lass.

MARY: No. Yo' mun tell me what it is.

ELLEN: Tha'll nobbut laugh at me.

MARY: No, no, A shan't. What were it?

ELLEN: It were a dream as got me oop, lass.

MARY: A dream!

ELLEN: Aye. *(Becoming incresingly terrified as she relates her dream.)*

A dreamed A were going in a field and the grass were green, greener than life, and theer was cows in it an' sheep – not dirty blackened beasties same as they are wi' us, but like as yo' might fancy they'd be somewheer where there isn't allays smoke. And A walked in th' field, and the sun were shining, an' it come dark sudden and A couldn't see the cows no more. Theer were thunder an' it frightened me; an' when A come to look up again it were raining blood on my yead. Nowt but blood, and the field ran red wi' it. Blood everywheer. Nowt but blood.

MARY: *(Sympathetically but relieved to find it no worse.)* An' it frightened thee? Aye, th' neeghtmare's noan pleasant for anybody. Yo' did eat a bit hearty last neeght. Well, never mind, it's all ower now. Tha'll feel better after a cup of tea. A'll soon have breakfast on table now.

ELLEN: *(Impressively, as if to herself rather than addressing MARY.)* A've dreamed yon dream afore, an' last time as A dreamed it were the neeght afore the big fire in the pit when Jack's father got 'isself killed. A've noan dreamed it sin' that neeght, and now it's coom again an' my boy's gone out to his work an' me too late to stop 'un.

MARY: *(Rushing to door C.)* Mebbe it's not too late.

ELLEN: *(As if awakened.)* Coom back, lass. *(Looking at clock.)* Look at clock. First cage 'ull be going down long afore tha could get theer, and our Jack 'ull be in it. He's allays in first cage our Jack. Best time-keeper on the pit.

MARY: *(Distractedly.)* Oh, why didn't yo' tell me at once? He'll be killed; he'll be killed.

ELLEN: *(Calmly.)* It's no use taking on like that. Jack's in God's keeping, lass, same as he is every day whether A dream or A don't. An' A dunno as theer's owt to trouble for. Folks do say as theer's nowt in dreams. A doubt it's going against th' Almighty to tak' notice of a dream: if He'd meant it for a warning, He'd happen 'ave sent it sooner so as A could have stopped Jack going out.

MARY: *(Calmed a little.)* Aye, he's in God's keeping. We can do nowt.

ELLEN: *(Briskly.)* Now. We're nowt but a pair o' silly wimmin to get skeered o' a dream. Don't thee take on about my whimsies. Coom now, bustle about. We'll never have breek fast today this road. Get kettle filled.

MARY: Yes, aunt.

ELLEN: *(Rising.)* A'll see to table.

MARY: All reeght.

ELLEN takes a coarse white cloth from a drawer in the table and spreads in, putting on it two cups and saucers, plates, and a brown teapot. MARY meantime lifts the kettle from the hob and goes out R. The sound of water pouring into the kettle is heard, and MARY returns and puts the kettle on the fire.

ELLEN: Put gas out, lass. It's leeght enough without now.

(MARY turns gas out. ELLEN sits before the fire. Reminiscently.)

Yo'll hardly mind an accident here, will yo', Mary?

MARY: No.

ELLEN: No. A thowt not. It's many a year sin' theer were 'un to speak of. A doan't call to mind as A've yeard the alarm bell ring more than onct or mebbe twict sin' your uncle were killed.

(With pride.)

11

That were summat like a do. Theer was about twenty killed that time, an' a matter o' forty or more as were hurt. Biggest accident as ever was in these parts were that 'un. A've yeard folks say as theer 'ave bin bigger do's in America, but A doan't tak' much notice o' them noospaper tales masel'. Eh, it might a' bin yesterday.

MARY: *(Sitting on the floor at ELLEN's feet.)* Tell me about it, aunt. You've never towld me how it chanced.

ELLEN: Eh? Bless the lass, what's good o' that? *(With energy.)* Seems to me we're both on us a bit crocked today. We's got accident on the brain.

MARY: *(Trying to draw her.)* They allays ring the bell, doan't they, aunt, when theer's owt goes wrong?

ELLEN: Not for an odd man an' 'is butty nipped in a roof-fall; only if it's a big thing. *(Pulling herself up.)* Sithee, lass, if tha canna talk o' nowt bar accidents, tha'd best shut tha faice. What wi' my dream an' thy worriting, A dunno wheer A am.

MARY: A were only asking. Theer's never no knowing wi' a coal-pit when it's going to turn awkward, an' a man canna remember allays wheer he is when he's down.

ELLEN: They're watched sharper going down nowadays, and the fellers knows better nor to tak' risks theirselves like they'd used to in th' ould days.

MARY: Aye. But a man as forgets onct 'ull forget onct too often.

ELLEN: *(Sharply.)* A've towld thee to quit moithering. Folks 'ud think tha'd noan lived aside pits beyond a week to hear thee talk silly like that. Theer's allays danger, an' no one bar a born fool 'ud say theer warn't, but it won't mend to goa thinking on't. Coal's theer and coal's got to be gotten, and that's top and bottom of it. Hast put tea in th' pot?

MARY: Naw. *(Rising.)*

ELLEN: Tha'd best do it then.

MARY puts tea in the teapot from a canister on the mantelpiece. As she does so, a bell outside is heard ringing violently.

MARY: *(Dropping the canister on the table.)* What's that?

The bell rings for a few moments, and ceases before ELLEN speaks.

ELLEN: *(Quietly and slowly, bending her head as if to a physical blow.)* God's will be done.

MARY: Is it –

ELLEN: *(Resignedly.)* Aye.

MARY makes for the door.

Wheer's tha going, lass?

MARY: *(Stopping, surprised at the question.)* A'm going to pit to see what's to do.

ELLEN: No, thou art not. A'll want thee here.

MARY: Why not?

ELLEN: *(Rising.)* Theer'll be enough fools o' wimmen theer seein' what's to do and hampering the men at theer work without yo're going and helping 'un to do it.

MARY: But we –

ELLEN: Sithee, lass, if our Jack's hurt, our job's to get 'un well again. Rushing off to pit-bank 'ull do 'un no good, unless mebbe tha's wanting to goa and get thy photo took an' see thy pretty face in paper same as Jack were showing us wi' yon pit as fell in soomwheer t'other day.

MARY: Yo' know A'm not.

ELLEN: No. Yon's noan our way. It's only wimmen as hasn't got husbands and sons down in th' pit as goes standing round fainting and what not and making a nuisance o' themselves. T'others stays at whoam an' gets things ready.

13

MARY: We doan't know what to get ready for.

ELLEN: We know enough.

MARY: Jack may not be hurt.

ELLEN: *(Dryly.)* Then us'll 'ave wasted our work.

MARY: *(Dully.)* What shall A do?

ELLEN: *(Looking round the room.)* A dunno as there's so much when all's done. We'll mebbe want hot water.

MARY: *(Shuddering.)* For –

ELLEN: *(Roughly.)* How do A know what for? *(Quietly looking round.)* Yon kettleful 'ull do, and our tea mun bide.

MARY: *(Distractedly.)* But what can we do? Give me summat to do, for mercy's sake. A'll goa mad if A doan't stir about. A can't sit still and wait, and wait, and wait. *(Her voice rises almost to a scream.)*

ELLEN: Tha's best be makkin' his bed.

MARY: *(Breaking down, tearfully.)* Yes, aunt.

ELLEN: What's thy crying for, lass? We doan't know nowt yet, and if we did, crying won't mend it. It 'ull do Jack no good, so how he is, to see thee slobbering when he cooms in.

MARY dries her eyes, sniffling, and begins to clear the table.

What's tha doing that for?

MARY: A dunno. A thowt –

ELLEN: Folks must eat. Leave things be. A towld thee to goa into his room and mak' his bed.

Exit MARY, L, closing the door behind her.

ELLEN looks to see that it is shut and then moves rapidly and purposefully to the door C. She throws it opens. It is now daylight. The confused murmur of a distant crowd is heard. She stands on the threshold and looks out. Presently she speaks to someone approaching, but not yet visible.

What is it, Polly?

POLLY LIVESEY, a middle-aged woman, in clogs, drab skirt and blouse, and with a shawl over her head and shoulders, appears breathless in the doorway.

POLLY: Ropes slipped and cage fell down shaft. Is yours gone out to work?

ELLEN: First cage down?

POLLY: Aye.

ELLEN: Mine's in it.

POLLY: We'll know worst soon. They was rigging tackle when A coom away. They'll have 'em up in no time.

ELLEN: A'll be ready. Wheer's yours?

POLLY: Mine's all reeght safe in theer beds, sleeping off last neeght's fuddle, thank the Lord.

ELLEN: They mun bring 'un here, Polly, so how he is.

POLLY: Aye. We all like to do for our own. Wheer's the lass? Gone to pit?

ELLEN: Makkin' 'is bed against he cooms.

POLLY: *(Approvingly.)* That's reeght. Doan't let her out.

ELLEN: Not if A can help it. She wanted to goa, but A wouldna have it. Theer's sights seen at pit-mouth arter an accident as isn't fit for a young 'un. Spoil her life for her to be theer when they're browt up.

POLLY: Aye. Am noan going back. A've had soom. Never no more if I can help it.

ELLEN: Coom in, wilta?

POLLY: Aye. A'd best close door, too, and keep noise out or she'll be wanting to go. *(Closes door. The murmur ceases.)*

ELLEN: Aye. They can't sit still when they're young.

POLLY: That's a fact. A recollect the day when the pit were afire. A were nobbut a young woman then, but my moother had no better sense not to let me out to pit-mouth to see the bodies browt up. A'll never forget that sight. A dream of it to this day.

ELLEN sits on the rocking-chair.

ELLEN: Sit thee down, Polly. A bit o' coompany cooms nicely at a time like this.

POLLY: *(Sitting.)* Thankee.

ELLEN: Aye, it's a thing yo' canna forget. Seems as it might be only t'other day as A yeard th' ould bell clang and saw my man browt oop. He were that charred A only knowed him by the earrings as he woore because his eyes was weak. They towld me arterwards as a hare had crossed his path on his road to the pit, but he were allays obstinate, were my Joe, and he wouldna tak' warning. And now the cage has slippit wi' my son in her and A'll have no manfolk now.

The door L. opens and MARY stands in the doorway. The others do not see her.

POLLY: Tha never knows. Mebbe he'll not be killed.

ELLEN: *(Hopelessly.)* A dreamt same dream last neeght as when his faither went.

POLLY: *(Quite convinced that hope is futile.)* In the midst o' life we are in death. Theer's no truer word nor that.

ELLEN: Not when yo' live by coal. Theer's wimmin as keeps house in the places th' coal goas to as pays for their coal wi' brass. We pay for it a sight heavier here. We pays wi' the lives o' men.

POLLY: *(Consoling her.)* But it's a comfort to think he'll noan be burned. A can't abide a corse that's burnt.

ELLEN: *(Agreeing.)* Aye, better broke than burnt.

POLLY: And tha'll have money in the burial club.

ELLEN: Oh aye. A can bury 'un proper.

POLLY: That's allays a comfort. Yo' doan't somehow seem to care so much when yo' know 'un's had a proper funeral. He's bin a good son to yo', an' all.

ELLEN: Oh aye, he's a good lad. He's mebbe had his shilling on a horse now and again and gone rattin' of a Sunday morning, but that's nobbut to say he's a man and not an angel in breeches.

POLLY: It's more than A can say wi' my lot. Lazy, drunken good-for-nowts they are, faither and sons alike. Coom to mention it, it's a rum thing. Providence goes to work its own way. If mine hadna been on spree last neeght they'd as like as not have bin in cage along o' your Jack.

MARY: *(Quietly.)* A'll go to pit now, aunt. *(She moves towards door C.)*

ELLEN: Wait your hurry, lass.

MARY: A can't wait. A mun know.

ELLEN: Sit thee down.

MARY: *(Feverishly.)* A can't sit down and hearken to yo' pair talking that road. First yo' get 'un killed and then yo' bury 'un, and next thing yo'll be debating what's to goa on's gravestone, and all the time yo' doan't so much as know if he's hurt.

POLLY: Sit thee still, lass. Tha'd best wait.

MARY: Oh, A dunno what yo're made of, yo' two. Yo' sit theer quiet and calm as if theer weren't nowt the matter.

ELLEN: We're owd enough to know we canna do no good. Hast made bed oop?

MARY: Aye.

ELLEN: Well, theer's a bottle o' brandy in th' cupboard in my room. We might need 'un.

MARY: A'll get it. *(Goes off briskly R.)*

POLLY: She's getting restless.

ELLEN: Aye. It cooms harder when yo're young to keep thasel' to thasel'. It doan't coom natural to her, not being born to pits, same as we was. Her moother was wed to a weaver chap in Blackburn and browt her oop to factories. It taks above a year or two to get into th' way o' the pits when yo're born foreign.

POLLY: Aye. We're used to thowt o' losing our men sudden.

ELLEN: But she's noan going to pit-mouth if A can stop her. We mun keep her a-gait. Is theer owt else we might want as yo' can think on?

POLLY: A dunno as theer is.

ELLEN: We might want linen fur tying up.

POLLY: No, yo'll not. Doctors were theer afore A coom away, and ambulance chaps, too, wi' all as they'll need. But we'll have to keep her here whether she likes it or not.

ELLEN: Aye. *(She looks towards the street-door. POLLY catches her meaning.)* Will yo'? A doan't move as easy as A used.

POLLY: The door?

ELLEN: Aye.

POLLY: Aye. That's reeght. *(She goes to the street door.)*

Better let her think we're ill usin' her than let her out to see them seeghts.

She turns the key and gives it to ELLEN as she resumes her seat.

ELLEN: Thankee, Polly. *(She pockets the key.)* Help me to mak' talk now and keep her mind off it.

MARY enters with a bottle.

MARY: There's the brandy.

ELLEN: That's reeght.

A slight pause; the older women try to make conversation. First POLLY bobs forward as if about to speak, but leans back without saying anything; ELLEN does the same. MARY moves to the door as ELLEN, glancing round for a subject, lets her eye fall on the brandy bottle and fires off her remark in time to arrest MARY's progress towards the door.

A thowt there was more than that in th' bottle, all th' same.

POLLY: It's a handy thing to have about th' house.

ELLEN: Aye. Rare stuff for th' jaw-ache.

POLLY: It is that. Goes well wi' a cup o' tea, too, on a cowld mornin'.

MARY: Is there anythin' else?

ELLEN: Eh? Nay, A doan't think there is Mary. Let me think. Nay. That's all A can mind.

MARY: A'll away, then.

ELLEN: No, yo'll not.

MARY: Why not?

ELLEN: Because yo'll not. Yo'll stay wheer y'are.

MARY: Let me go. A mun go. A canna stay 'ere.

POLLY: Do what th' aunt tells thee, lass. Young folks is that smart, nowadays, there's no use tellin' them anythin'.

MARY: Oh, yo' doan't understand. A mun go. A mun.

She goes to the door; tries to open it.

Door's locked. This door's locked. Wheer's th' key? What have yo' done wi' th' key?

ELLEN: Look here, lass, A towld yo' ye wouldn't goa, an' A've made sure o' it. Coom now. Coom an' sit quiet, ravin' about as if yo' were mad. Yo'll have th' handle off door.

MARY: Let me goa to 'im.

ELLEN: No.

MARY: A mun go. A mun. A love 'im. A love 'im.

ELLEN: Dost tha think A doan't love 'im, lass? Aye and a seeght better than a bit lass like yo' could love 'im. A'm 'is moother.

MARY: Oh, have mercy. Yo' doan't know. A sent 'im out. He wasn't for goin' till A'd said th' word. A wouldn't tell 'im. A made 'im wait till th' neeght. A sent 'im to 'is death.

ELLEN: The lass's ravin'.

MARY: Let me go.

ELLEN: No.

MARY: Tha won't?

POLLY: Hold tha wish, lass. It's for tha own good.

MARY: Why hast tha locked the door? Yo're cheatin' me. Yo're cruel. A can do no good 'ere. Let me goa to 'im. A mun go. A will.

Approaching ELLEN: the two women face each other for a moment. Suddenly there is a loud kicking at the door.

What's that? Oh my God, what's that?

ELLEN takes the key from her pocket and slowly moves to the door. She inserts the key and throws the door open. JACK stands on the doorstep, his coat buttoned at the bottom and with his right arm thrust into it.

ELLEN: My lad. *(She tries to embrace him.)*

JACK: *(Holding her off with his left arm.)* Steady on, moother. Mind my arm.

ELLEN: Is't broke?

JACK: Aye. Doctor'll be round to set 'un soon. They've gotten enough to do first, though. Theer's plenty worse than me. *(He comes in and sits in the rocking-chair.)*

ELLEN: Thank God! *(She covers her face with her hands.)*

JACK: Nay, moother. It's all ower. Theer's nowt to cry for, and not so much in a brokken arm to thank God for, neither. *(He puts his uninjured hand upon her shoulder.)*

Well, lass. *(Looking at MARY.)*

MARY: Oh, Jack!

JACK: Is that all as tha's got to say to me? Shift's ower, lass. Mebbe it's ower afore it's begun, but that'll noan matter. A've coom fur my answer, lass.

MARY: Tha owd soft. Tha knew all time. Oh, Jack, Jack, A thowt tha was killed.

JACK: Tha thowt wrong. A'm noan th' dying sort. So tha'll have me.

MARY: Aye.

JACK: A'll goa round an' see parson about putting up th' banns when my arm's set. A'll be having soom time on my hands. I reckon getting wed 'ull fill 'un in nicely.

End.

NIGHT WATCHES
BY ALLAN MONKHOUSE

An ante-room to the wards in a small Red Cross Hospital. The door is at the back and it leads to a landing out of which the wards – a large and a small bedroom – open. In the room are a clock showing clearly the time – a few minutes after ten – a fire with an armchair before it, a coal scuttle, a low camp bed covered with a blanket, a small table in which is a tray covered with a table-cloth, a stand with a spirit lamp and a kettle, etc. A NURSE enters with the NIGHT-ORDERLY. He is an ordinary citizen of middle age; she is a comely woman of middle age.

NURSE: This your room. Plenty of coal, I think? It gets rather chilly in the middle of the night.

ORDERLY: Thank you very much. What about that bed? Am I supposed to go to sleep?

NURSE: Oh, I think so. Unless you're a very heavy sleeper. Of course, you make your rounds every two or three hours. But you'll find all quiet, I think. We've no troublesome cases – unless – no, I don't think you'll be disturbed.

ORDERLY: *(Pointing to the tray.)* What's that?

NURSE: That's your tray.

She half uncovers it, displaying teapot, loaf, etc.

There are biscuits in this paper bag.

ORDERLY: I shan't want anything.

NURSE: Yes, they all say that at first.

ORDERLY: No, but really

NURSE: Here's the tea-caddy.

ORDERLY: I never take anything after dinner.

NURSE: And here's the toasting fork.

ORDERLY: I don't think I shall want it.

NURSE: *(Looking at the kettle.)* You'd better light this spirit lamp in good time. It takes some time to boil. Or you could use the fire.

25

ORDERLY: You're very good. But…

NURSE: If you can spend a night with a good cup of tea staring at you you're very different from most people.

ORDERLY: *(Relenting.)* Oh, I'm quite an ordinary person.

NURSE: Yes; most people are.

ORDERLY: I do rather like the idea of a round of hot buttered toast.

NURSE: I don't think you'll be satisfied with the idea.

ORDERLY: Perhaps not. Well, nurse, what are my instructions?

NURSE: You'd better read that paper on the wall.

ORDERLY: I see.

NURSE: The door just opposite is the big ward. Eight of them there. The little ward is the room at the end of the passage to the right. *(She indicates to it.)* Only two in that. They've been getting a little restless. I'm not sure that we shan't have to make a change there.

ORDERLY: What sort of a change?

NURSE: Well, we might put one of them in the big ward and somebody else in there. I think they're getting a bit on one another's nerves those two. One of them's the deaf and dumb man, you know. You'd better have a look at him when you go round. But he's near the bell.

ORDERLY: A deaf and dumb man?

NURSE: Dreadful, isn't it? A shell burst near him; he wasn't wounded but he can't speak a word now and can't hear.

ORDERLY: Will he get right?

NURSE: They hope so. There's a chance.

ORDERLY: Well, you're sure I needn't keep awake all the time?

NURSE: I don't think you will.

ORDERLY: I'll spend the night pinching myself if you tell me to.

NURSE: Do it if you like.

ORDERLY: You're not going?

NURSE: Yes.

ORDERLY: Won't you sit down and have half-an-hour's chat? Have a cup of tea?

NURSE: *(Shakes her head smilingly.)* If there's anything wrong, anything you can't tackle, call me. There's a bell we've rigged up here to my room. See? I think you've got every thing. Good night.

ORDERLY: Good night, nurse. Thank you.

NURSE: *(Stands at the door, listening.)* They are all sleeping. Poor boys, poor boys.

She goes. The ORDERLY looks after her wistfully. He takes a turn about the room, examines the toasting-fork, takes up a book, puts it down, sits in the armchair and begins to fill his pipe thoughtfully.

Some time passes.

The ORDERLY is dozing in the chair and the clock shows that it is half-past two. He rouses gradually and listens. A SOLDIER pushes the door open and looks in. His dress is a rough compromise between day and night. His is youngish, a typical private, now rather perturbed. His head is bandaged.

ORDERLY: What's up now?

SOLDIER 1: 'Scuse me, sir.

He salutes.

May I have a word with you, sir?

ORDERLY: Certainly. Come in.

SOLDIER 1: *(Advancing.)* I didn't ought to be put in there with 'im.

ORDERLY: In where? With whom?

SOLDIER 1: Little ward, they call it. There's only two of us: me an' 'im.

ORDERLY: Little ward? Well, but there's a deaf and dumb man there. He can't disturb you.

SOLDIER 1: Can't he?

ORDERLY: How can he if he's but perhaps you're the deaf and dumb man?

SOLDIER 1: *(Laughs uneasily.)* About as much as 'e is.

ORDERLY: Do you mean to say that he's shamming?

SOLDIER 1: I didn't say that. But he might be pretendin'.

ORDERLY: He might be? What's the difference?

SOLDIER 1: Well, one's worse than the other, isn't it?

ORDERLY: D'you think so? Shamming sounds worse, doesn't it?

SOLDIER 1: Of course it does. I'd never say a man was shammin' unless I knew. It wouldn't be fair.

ORDERLY: But you'd say he was pretending? Well, now, that's interesting. Sit down and explain the difference. Have a cigarette?

SOLDIER 1: Thanky, sir.

He takes one and sits down.

ORDERLY: Now, then.

SOLDIER 1: They wanted to get 'im out o' that big ward an' they did.

ORDERLY: Did they? Why?

SOLDIER 1: Deaf an' dumb is 'e?

ORDERLY: Well, isn't he?

SOLDIER 1: Shall I tell y' somethin', sir?

ORDERLY: Do.

SOLDIER 1: I'm not one to blab.

ORDERLY: No; don't blab. Just tell me.

SOLDIER 1: What shall I tell y'?

ORDERLY: Oh, heavens! Tell me the difference between shamming and pretending.

SOLDIER 1: It's a rum thing. I never thought he was that sort of feller.

ORDERLY: What sort?

SOLDIER 1: You think it's only pretendin'?

ORDERLY: What's only pretending?

SOLDIER 1: Shall I tell y'?

ORDERLY: No; not unless you like. Don't tell me anything. Go to bed.

SOLDIER 1: I'm bound to tell y'.

ORDERLY: Fire away, then.

SOLDIER 1: Calls himself deaf and dumb?

ORDERLY: Does he? Funny that he should call himself anything.

SOLDIER 1: He can talk right enough.

ORDERLY: How d'you know?

SOLDIER 1: I've heard him. Others too. That's what they didn't like. Them in the big ward.

ORDERLY: When have you heard him?

SOLDIER 1: *(Impressively.)* In his sleep.

29

ORDERLY: I see. I see.

SOLDIER 1: Thought y'd see.

ORDERLY: Has he done it often?

SOLDIER 1: Pretty reg'lar.

ORDERLY: Can you make out what he says?

SOLDIER 1: No, he's a bit too clever for that.

ORDERLY: Too clever? Oh, come. How can that be?

SOLDIER 1: Looks like pretendin'? What?

ORDERLY: And why not shamming? Why don't you call it shamming?

SOLDIER 1: I'll tell y'. Because he's deaf right enough.

ORDERLY: How d'you know?

SOLDIER 1: 'Cause y' may make a noise like hell behind 'im and he doesn't move. Y' may burst a paper bag agen 'is ear 'ole. He's deaf, 'e is, so I wouldn't go so far as to say 'e's shammin'.

ORDERLY: Yes, I begin to see the difference.

SOLDIER 1: Thought y' would.

ORDERLY: Now, look here. I don't think he's shamming or pretending or anything.

SOLDIER 1: I tell y' I've 'eard 'im many a time. It used to make me go creeps. It does still but I'm more vexed now. When y' curse 'im for it he can't 'ear a word.

ORDERLY: Look here. Have you – any of you – told him that he talks in his sleep?

SOLDIER 1: Tell 'im? 'E wouldn't 'ear.

ORDERLY: Yes, yes, yes; but you can write it. He can read, I suppose?

SOLDIER 1: I don't set much store by that way of writin'.

ORDERLY: Now, that's no reason.

SOLDIER 1: I don't want 'im on to me.

ORDERLY: What d'you mean ?

SOLDIER 1: You don't know what a feller like that'll do.

ORDERLY: What have you against him?

SOLDIER 1: *(Testily.)* 'Aven't I been tellin' y'?

ORDERLY: Not a word.

SOLDIER 1: Are you off your nut or am I?

ORDERLY: Both of us, perhaps.

SOLDIER 1: He gives out as 'e's dumb. Is 'e?

ORDERLY: Yes. When he's awake.

SOLDIER 1: Well, now.

ORDERLY: Let me explain or try to. What is this dumbness? He has had a great shock and it has completely shattered – paralysed – of course, I don't understand it as a doctor would or a scientific man – it has put all his nerves wrong, it has cut off – or paralysed – the connections between his will – what he wants to do and what he can do. D'you see? Well, he's all, as it were, dithering. And then he goes to sleep.

SOLDIER 1: Ah! That's it.

ORDERLY: *(Encouraged.)* He goes to sleep. And do you know – have you thought what a beautiful thing sleep is? We relax, we sink into nature, we – you don't read Shakespeare?

SOLDIER 1: I've 'eard tell of 'im.

ORDERLY: Well, he once wrote a play about a murderer.

SOLDIER 1: *(Starting.)* A murderer!

ORDERLY: Yes; and when this murderer knew that he would never sleep peacefully again he reeled off the most beautiful praises of sleep and what sleep could do – devil take you, I believe you're too stupid to understand.

SOLDIER 1: I'll understand if you'll talk sense.

ORDERLY: Yes. I beg your pardon. It's my fault. Well, sleep will do wonders. It will heal you, it will put things right for the time, it will help you to put them right altogether. It accomplishes miracles. You awake – and there you are again.

SOLDIER 1: D'you believe all this yourself, sir?

ORDERLY: I think so. Yes.

SOLDIER 1: You said a murderer.

ORDERLY: That was Macbeth. A chap called Macbeth.

SOLDIER 1: Talked in 'is sleep, did 'e?

ORDERLY: Well, his wife did. She was a murderer too.

SOLDIER 1: Yes, you may be sure there's summat wrong when they do that.

ORDERLY: No, no. The most innocent people may do it.

SOLDIER 1: Innercent, indeed! He's got a bad conscience, that chap.

ORDERLY: What is a bad conscience? It's only an uncomfortable mind. Most of you have that. Most of us, I should say.

SOLDIER 1: Are y' sayin' I've a bad conscience?

ORDERLY: No; but I can believe that if you've been out to the war and seen horrible things you may have them on your mind. You may even talk in your sleep.

SOLDIER 1: That's a lie.

ORDERLY: You mustn't speak to me like that.

SOLDIER 1: *(Saluting.)* Beg y'r pard'n, sir.

ORDERLY: I'm not making myself out any better than you. I've a bad conscience.

SOLDIER 1: You, sir?

ORDERLY: Oh, this war finds us out. All the things that we might have done or left undone.

SOLDIER 1: D'you talk in y'r sleep?

ORDERLY: *(Laughing.)* Oh! I won't admit that.

SOLDIER 1: I sh'd think not.

ORDERLY: Now, look here. You're a fair-minded man. What have you against this poor chap in your room? Just look at it calmly as if you were judge or jury. What has he done?

SOLDIER 1: Y' talk of 'orrible things. I've seen some and I don't mention 'em – we tell y' a lot but there are some things – we may 'av seen 'em or – we may 'av thought 'em. Better forget; better forget.

ORDERLY: Well, my dear fellow, that's just it. That should make you sympathise with him.

SOLDIER 1: Or we may 'av done 'em.

ORDERLY: Yes, I see.

SOLDIER 1: Y' can't be sure. Of anyone else I mean.

ORDERLY: Of course you can't. You can't be sure of anything. But you musn't condemn others.

SOLDIER 1: What 'as that feller seen? What 'as he done? I'm alone with 'im in that little ward. I can't make out a word, but it's talkin' right enough. I've stood over 'im listenin'. It's 'orrible langwidge. I can't make out a word. 'Ardly.

ORDERLY: Oh! come, you know

SOLDIER 1: He's done somethin'. I know 'e 'as.

ORDERLY: Oh, well, my friend, if it comes to that you've done a bit of killing or tried to.

SOLDIER 1: I 'ad to kill them bloody Germans.

ORDERLY: I know that. That's all right.

SOLDIER 1: It's all so 'orrible sir that you want things to be done right. You don't want any 'anky–panky.

ORDERLY: Yes, I see.

SOLDIER 1: Them Germans! I reckon they're all like 'im.

ORDERLY: How like him?

SOLDIER 1: All talkin' in their sleep.

ORDERLY: That's a dreadful idea.

SOLDIER 1: An' there am I with 'im in the night. And in the big ward they're sleepin' peaceful. What did that Shakespeare say of sleep?

ORDERLY: He said a lot of things.

SOLDIER 1: Tell me one.

ORDERLY: The death of each day's life.

SOLDIER 1: An 'orrible idea. Damn 'im.

ORDERLY: You musn't damn Shakespeare.

SOLDIER 1: I will if 'e talks like that. No disrespec' to you sir. What else did 'e say?

ORDERLY: Sore labour's bath,
Balm of hurt minds, great nature's second course,
Chief nourisher in life's feast.

SOLDIER 1: *(Humbly.)* I don't understand.

(Resentfully.) Why, it might be 'im talkin' in 'is sleep. *(He jerks his thumb.)*

ORDERLY: Yes, he may be saying the most beautiful things.

SOLDIER 1: Nay, 'e's a devil, that feller is.

ORDERLY: Hullo! What's that?

SOLDIER 1: Begod, 'e's comin'.

They both look towards the door and the SECOND SOLDIER appears there. He stands surveying them timidly and yet morosely. He wears an old dressing-gown over pyjamas.

ORDERLY: This is most irregular. I shall get into a row.

Seeing him speak the SECOND SOLDIER straightens himself and salutes. Then he advances slowly into the room.

SOLDIER 1: *(In a stentorian voice.)* Y're on fire.

The SECOND SOLDIER takes no notice.

ORDERLY: What the dickens d'you mean? You'll wake everybody.

SOLDIER 1: It's all right, sir. Best try 'im now and then. He might get back 'is 'earin' sudden. I think y' may talk free before 'im now.

ORDERLY: I don't know that I want to talk before him. I want you both to go back to bed.

SOLDIER 1: I'm not goin' back before 'e does.

ORDERLY: Why?

SOLDIER 1: Lyin' there in the dark and thinkin' 'e may come in.

The SECOND SOLDIER makes a gesture to indicate that he wants the other sent away. It is intended to be surreptitious, but the FIRST SOLDIER observes.

Look at that! See 'im? No, you don't.

35

The SECOND SOLDIER fumbles in the pockets of his gown and produces a small slate and a pencil. He writes. The FIRST SOLDIER tries to see what he is writing, and there is a mild scuffle. The SECOND SOLDIER seeks the protection of the ORDERLY, who overlooks his writing and waves the FIRST SOLDIER away.

Fair do's.

ORDERLY: Let him write.

SOLDIER 1: Yes, but let me see it.

ORDERLY: Why should you?

SOLDIER 1: 'Tisn't polite to whisper in company.

ORDERLY: Whisper?

SOLDIER 1: Same thing if you don't let me look.

ORDERLY: Well, the fact is he wants a little private conversation with me.

SOLDIER 1: Oh! Indeed! Wants me to go? Well, I'm not 'aving any. That's straight.

ORDERLY: If I tell you to go you'll have to.

SOLDIER 1: Cert'nly, sir; but he oughtn't to write about me be'ind my back.

ORDERLY: You've been talking about him behind his back.

SOLDIER 1: Yes, but he couldn't 'ear any 'ow.

ORDERLY: What's that to do with it?

SOLDIER 1: An' I can read writin'.

ORDERLY: Your distinctions are too fine for me.

The SECOND SOLDIER has been writing on the slate and now hands it to the ORDERLY who reads and laughs.

SOLDIER 1: What's he say?

ORDERLY: He says you're very restless and he thinks you have something on your mind.

SOLDIER 1: Well, I never.

ORDERLY: He says he doesn't know what you've been doing, but you must have a bad conscience.

SOLDIER 1: 'e's like them Germans. They always say as it's us does their dirty tricks. P'raps 'e is one.

ORDERLY: Now, you've no right to say that.

SOLDIER 1: No, sir; I 'aven't.

The SECOND SOLDIER grasps the slate again, rubs out his messages with fingers moistened at his mouth and writes eagerly. The FIRST SOLDIER manages to look over. He backs away.

(Feebly.) 'e says I'm a bad man.

ORDERLY: *(Looking at the slate as the SECOND SOLDIER writes.)* He says he caught you bending over him and going to stick something in him.

SOLDIER 1: 'e's a liar.

ORDERLY: And that you must be sent away.

SOLDIER 1: I'll bash 'is 'ed in.

ORDERLY: Silence.

The TWO SOLDIERS glare at one another snarling and menacing. The ORDERLY steps between.

SOLDIER 1: If 'e wants a scrap I'm 'is man.

ORDERLY: You two fools.

(To THE FIRST SOLDIER.) You should be sorry for the poor fellow. It's the old tale. Fear breeds cruelty.

SOLDIER 1: Fear!

ORDERLY: Yes, fear. You're brave enough when it comes to killing Germans, I daresay, but you're afraid of nothing at all. There's something here you can't understand, and, like a coward, you blame this poor fellow. You should help him. He's your comrade – your pal. It's the way with all of us. We fear and fear and then we'll do any beastly cruel thing.

He takes the slate and pencil and begins to write.

SOLDIER 1: *(Sullenly.)* What'r y' tellin' 'im?

ORDERLY: Very much what I've been saying to you.

SOLDIER 1: I 'aven't touched 'im.

ORDERLY: Why! If you two fellows were back in the trenches together you'd die for one another.

He gives the slate to the SECOND SOLDIER, who reads, grabs the pencil, turns to the other side of the slate and writes furiously.

SOLDIER 1: I dessay. What's 'e writin' now?

ORDERLY: I don't know.

The SECOND SOLDIER throws the slate on the table and moves towards the door. The FIRST SOLDIER tries to get it, but the orderly is before him.

SOLDIER 1: What's 'e say?

ORDERLY: *(Angrily in a loud voice to SECOND SOLDIER after reading.)* Don't be a fool. Deuce take it, I'm forgetting now.

SOLDIER 1: What does 'e say?

ORDERLY: He says he'll blow his brains out.

SOLDIER 1: *(Daunted.)* I don't wish 'im no 'arm. Not a bit.

The ORDERLY gets hold of the SECOND SOLDIER and leads him forward to a chair toward the front, where he sits down dejectedly. The ORDERLY picks up the slate.

ORDERLY: Where's that pencil?

As he is looking for it the first soldier, who has been in a state of uncomfortable hesitancy, approaches the SECOND SOLDIER from behind and brings his mouth close to the other's ear.

SOLDIER 1: *(In a terrific voice.)* Bill!

The SECOND SOLDIER starts slightly and then rises unsteadily. He turns slowly to look at the FIRST SOLDIER.

(In an awed voice.) 'e 'eard me.

Trembling, the SECOND SOLDIER stretches out his hand for the slate. The ORDERLY hands him the pencil and he tries to write, but his agitation overcomes him and he sits down. In the meantime the FIRST SOLDIER empties the bag of biscuits and again approaches the SECOND SOLDIER, this time blowing out the bag into a balloon. He explodes it at ear of the SECOND SOLDIER, who rises again and sees the torn bag. With an inarticulate cry he falls on the neck of the first soldier.

I made 'im 'ear.

They waltz round the room together and passing the ORDERLY drag him in. He joins in the dance and they knock over a chair or two. The NURSE, in a dressing-gown, enters.

NURSE: Well!

They separate, looking rather sheepish, but the FIRST SOLDIER soon recovers and cautiously gets hold of the poker and tongs.

ORDERLY: You've caught us this time, nurse.

NURSE: Whatever are you doing; you'll wake everybody. Really, sir.

ORDERLY: Oh, you must forgive us, nurse. There's been a great reconciliation. And more than that.

The SECOND SOLDIER seizes the NURSE's arm. He simulates shouting, taps his ears and gesticulates explanations and delight.

NURSE: Can he hear?

ORDERLY: Not much yet, but something.

The FIRST SOLDIER makes a sudden and great clanging with the fire-irons.

NURSE: Whatever's that?

ORDERLY: Stop, confound you.

SOLDIER 1: Give 'im a bit o' pleasure.

The two SOLDIERS shake hands.

NURSE: Well, I don't know what to say. It's most irregular.

ORDERLY: Report us, nurse; report us. Blame me.

SOLDIER 1: *(Confidently, to orderly.)* 'E's not 'alf a bad chap.

The two SOLDIERS shake hands.

NURSE: Now, you two be off to bed.

(She gesticulates to the SECOND SOLDIER.)

Where's his slate? The pencil?

SOLDIER 1: Oh, never mind that! 'E'll be talkin' d'rectly. 'E talks in 'is sleep now. My Gawd! I used to be frightened of 'im. At nights you get thinkin'.

NURSE: Well, be off, be off, that's good boys.

They start off arm in arm.

SOLDIER 1: *(Turning.)* What time may I start talkin' to 'im?

NURSE: What time?

SOLDIER 1: Yes, I'm goin' to make 'im 'ear proper in the mornin'.

NURSE: I'll box your ears if I hear a sound before eight o'clock.

SOLDIER 1: Well, look out then.

They go off laughing.

ORDERLY: You'll have to report me.

NURSE: Shall I?

ORDERLY: Won't you? We must have awakened all of them?

NURSE: It wasn't quite so bad as shells bursting, after all.

ORDERLY: Well, do you want a full explanation?

NURSE: It'll do in the morning. You can make a report. But I think I know.

She goes to the door and listens.

They're all sleeping quietly.

ORDERLY: Good lads!

NURSE: They've all sorts of fancies. They're so different in the daytime. Now – they're breathing like one. Even those two – very soon they'll be asleep.

ORDERLY: We're groping among strange things, nurse.

NURSE: I don't know that I understand you. They're like children to me. These two naughty ones – well, you know what I mean.

ORDERLY: Do I? Don't let us understand everything.

NURSE: Good night, again.

ORDERLY: Good night, nurse.

NURSE: *(Going.)* You have a cup of tea now and that toast.

ORDERLY: Am I one of your children too?

NURSE: Are you wounded and ill?

ORDERLY: No; only rather melancholy.

NURSE: *(She shakes her head.)* Try a cup of tea.

She goes out. The ORDERLY gazes after her. Then he lifts up the teapot and looks at it.

INTERVAL

THE OLD TESTAMENT AND THE NEW
BY STANLEY HOUGHTON

The Scene is laid in the South Cheshire country town of Danesbridge. It is a late autumn evening, chilly and wet. The stage represents an old-fashioned room with wooden beams across the ceiling and walls half panelled. In the middle of the back wall is a large bay window, the panes covered with dark green curtains. Nearest the spectator, on his left, is a door leading to the other part of the house, and farther away a large fireplace. In the back, to the right of the window, is a door opening into a small hall. From this hall the outer door, which is visible, opens onto the street.

In the hall is a hat stand with a coat, a couple of hats, and an umbrella. An old-fashioned bureau, on which there is a large worn Bible, books, papers, and a file of bills, stands in the bay window. On the wall to the right of the spectator a large dresser-sideboard, bearing some old blue and white pottery. By the fire an armchair, another chair, and a small table covered with papers, books, pen and ink. In the centre of the stage a large oval dining-table covered with a green, gold and brown cloth. The half nearest the door is spread with a white tray cloth, and supper for one is laid. There are a piece of cheese, a cottage loaf, butter, a knife and spoon, a plate, a glass jug of water, and a tumbler. Three chairs surround the table. A grandfather clock stands at the back and left of the window opening. The furniture is mahogany and horsehair, comfortable and well used. The pictures are hunting-scene engravings of Landseer's in old gilt frames, and there is a framed testimonial hung over the mantelpiece. A lighted oil-lamp is on the sideboard, and another on the bureau. There is a chair by the door in the hall.

When the curtain rises, CHRISTOPHER and MARTHA Battersby are in the room. CHRISTOPHER is a powerfully built man of rather under average height, with a sleight stoop. His face is resolute and well lined. He has a firm jaw, with a small, close-cut chin beard. His hair has been sandy brown, but is now nearly iron-grey. He looks more than his age, which is about sixty-three. He is soberly dressed in a rather old-fashioned suit.

MARTHA is nearly the same height as her husband. She wears black with a quaint cap and apron. Her hair is of a dead white, and her face, which is sweet though not strong, bears a sad expression. She is about sixty, but looks more.

CHRISTOPHER is working at a small table near the fire. He is occupied with a mass of papers and books and seems puzzled. MARTHA has just finished laying the table. She watches CHRISTOPHER.

MARTHA: You're looking worried, Christopher. What's amiss?

CHRIS: Eh?

MARTHA: You're looking worried.

CHRIS: Ay, I'm a bit puzzled. It's these accounts for furnishing the minister's house. I don't understand them altogether.

MARTHA: Put them by for to-night. Edward will be here soon.

CHRIS: Ay, ay, so he will. It's past nine. He'll be able to aid me, likely.

MARTHA: Now as if Edward would understand anything about the chapel books.

CHRIS: Why not? He is a commercial traveller; he must know something about accounts.

MARTHA: Ay, business accounts, not chapel. They're not the same. Besides, the lad'll be weary. Bear in mind he's comin' all the way from Nottingham.

CHRIS: So he will. And hungry. Have ye got him some supper ready?

MARTHA: There's a nice new bit o' cheese, and some soup keeping hot in the kitchen.

CHRIS: That's right. I want Edward to feel at home when he comes here.

MARTHA: Now let me side them papers and things away. I don't feel comfortable with the place so untidy.

CHRIS: Let them be till I've done, Martha; and then I'll side them myself. I'd rather. I don't know where to look for things when you've put them tidy.

MARTHA: As you please.

CHRIS: I'll have to see Mr. Dove about these in the mornin'. I doubt I'm getting too old for Circuit Steward.

MARTHA: Too old indeed! You're tired to-night, that's all.

CHRIS: *(Goes to bureau to consult a file of papers.)* Ay, perhaps I am. I'd a long walk this forenoon to Jacob Bowers.

MARTHA: *(Sitting by fire.)* And how is he?

CHRIS: Poorly, poorly – and the bailiff's threatening again.

MARTHA: Ay. Did you?

CHRIS: I lent him five pounds, Martha. It's a deal o' money, but he's a chapel member – and we've no other use for our money now.

MARTHA: Don't say that, Christopher.

CHRIS: *(Rapping on bureau.)* Now, now! We'll not talk of that.

MARTHA sighs. CHRISTOPHER comes back to his table and applies himself to his work. A slight pause.

Surely Edward should be here now.

MARTHA: Likely the train's late. Doesn't it seem good to have him coming again? Sometimes I feel as though he was really our own son.

CHRIS: Ay, he's a good lad; though he never was so fond of the chapel.

MARTHA: Eh, but to think of what might have been if Providence hadn't ordained things otherwise. He might have been bringing the lass with him.

CHRIS: Martha! We'll not speak of that, neither.

MARTHA: No, you never will.

CHRIS: No. And I'll not have you speak of it. She's gone, and she's not to be mentioned.

MARTHA: *(Sighing.)* Very well, Christopher.

47

A long pause. MARTHA dabs her eyes with a handkerchief, and CHRISTOPHER wrinkles his brow over his work. A knock is heard at the door.

MARTHA: That'll be Edward. *(She hurries to the door.)*

CHRIS: *(Looking up.)* Ay. *(He resumes his work.)*

MARTHA opens the door, showing the hall, and then opens the outer door. EDWARD in coat and hat comes into the hall. He is an easy, comfortable-looking man of about twenty-eight, inclined to stoutness, with a good-natured, weak, and rather red face, and a slight sandy moustache. Altogether he seems rather commonplace.

EDWARD: Well, mother, and how are you?

She is about to kiss him.

No, wait a bit. My coat's wet. It's raining.

He hangs his coat on a hook in the hall.

Now then.

MARTHA: *(Kissing him.)* My dear lad. But if your coat's wet, and it is that, it mustn't stay here. I'll put it before t' fire to dry. *(She takes it.)*

EDWARD: You're very good. Father in, eh?

He enters room followed by MARTHA.

MARTHA: Ay, he's in, and a rare mess he's making with his books and papers and what-not all over the place. But it's no use talking to him.

CHRIS: *(Rising.)* Now, Martha, stop your chattering. Well, lad, so you're in Danesbridge agen. *(Places his hand on EDWARD's shoulder.)*

EDWARD: Yes. But I'm only here for to-night. We've not done much business in Danesbridge of late, and trade's so bad now I can't waste time. I've to call at Bollinwich, Port Stock, and Wirkchester to-morrow.

MARTHA puts coat to dry on chair by fire and goes out into the kitchen.

CHRIS: Well, well, sit down. There's a bit of supper waiting for ye. Have ye no luggage?

EDWARD: There's my bag and a skip of samples. The outporter's bringing them on. He'll be round in half an hour or so.

CHRIS: Ah! I'm just a bit bothered with these chapel accounts. I suppose ye'd not care to help me with them, eh? Too tired?

EDWARD: Well – I can't say I'm keen on it just now.

CHRIS: All right! all right! I'll leave them tonight.

EDWARD: You don't mind?

CHRIS: Not a bit, lad, not a bit.

He gathers up the papers and puts them on the bureau. EDWARD crosses to the fire and stands with his back to it.

Enter MARTHA.

MARTHA: Christopher, you never thought to get that beer in for Edward.

CHRIS: Eh, no! It went clean out of my head. We don't drink it, as you know, Edward; but I'm a broad-minded man. I don't object to it in moderation. Would ye like a bottle?

EDWARD: I wouldn't mind one. There's not much body in water.

MARTHA: I thought he would.

CHRIS: I'll run out to the Rose and Lion for one.

EDWARD: You're very good.

CHRIS: My coat's in the lobby, eh, Martha?

MARTHA: On the hook.

CHRIS goes out and closes door. Shortly after the noise of the outer door closing is heard.

MARTHA: Well, Edward, it's good to see you again. How are your mother and sisters?

EDWARD: Oh, I think they're all right.

MARTHA: Think! You ought to know. You've just left them.

EDWARD: Eh. Yes – of course. Oh, they're very well. Mother sent her love.

MARTHA: Thank you. Give her mine when you get home. Eh, it seems a long time since you all left here.

EDWARD: It's just over two years.

MARTHA: Two years. Ah! And you still like Nottingham?

EDWARD: Fairly. But there's no question of liking. My getting the place as traveller at the lace factory meant living there, and there was no help for it.

MARTHA: And such a blow to me it was, your going, Edward. You don't know how lonely I feel at times. I'd got to look on you as a son, as you should have been by now.

EDWARD: You oughtn't to be lonely. I'm sure he's good enough to you. *(Nods towards door through which CHRISTOPHER has gone.)* Cheer up!

MARTHA: Oh, he's kind enough. But he's bound up in the chapel. I'm not so fond of it as he is. Sometimes *(She looks around fearfully.)* I think they're not Christian enough at the chapel. They preach too much out of the Old Testament.

EDWARD: Well, it's all one. *(Laughing.)* All the same book, eh?

MARTHA: No. The Old Testament's so much crueller than the New. But that's not all. Christopher's good to me – but it's a child's love I want. Living here's been like living in a house without windows since – since.

EDWARD: Ay.

MARTHA: Since Mary went away. The light's all gone out of the house.

EDWARD: Mr. Battersby – doesn't he speak of her?

MARTHA: Never a word.

EDWARD: And you've never heard anything of her?

MARTHA: No.

EDWARD: Ah, I'm sorry for you.

MARTHA: It's very good of you to come and stay with us when you visit Danesbridge. It comforts me a good deal. And she going and leaving you the week before you should have been wed!

EDWARD: *(Getting uncomfortable.)* 'm, yes.

MARTHA: And you loved her so.

EDWARD: Oh ay – I did.

MARTHA: And you still love her?

EDWARD: 'm – well – I've told you so many a time, mother, haven't I?

MARTHA: Ay, ay. But I like you to tell me every time, lest you may have changed.

EDWARD: Well – I've – I've not – I've not.

MARTHA: And you'd still marry her if she came back?

EDWARD grimaces to himself and scratches his head.

You would?

EDWARD: There's not much fear of her coming back now.

MARTHA: She may. I pray for it every day. You'd still marry her?

EDWARD: Haven't I told you so many a time?

MARTHA: But you've not altered? You would still?

EDWARD: *(Uncomfortable.)* Oh, yes, yes, yes, of course, mother. *(He kisses her.)* Don't worry about that.

MARTHA: Oh, I'm thankful. There's just that that's keeping me up still. The chance that she may come back and live happy with you, and that Christopher'll forgive her. It's something to live for. *(She wipes her eyes.)*

EDWARD: Let's hope so. Let's hope so, mother.

The door opens and CHRIS, appears with a bottle of Bass.

CHRIS: I've been a long time, haven't I? I met the minister just as I was coming out of the Rose and Lion with the bottle under my arm. He looked a bit taken aback, so I had to stop and explain. He's not so broad-minded as I am.

EDWARD laughs heartily.

MARTHA: Dear, dear! Have you fastened the front door?

CHRIS: No; I've left it on the latch. There's Edward's luggage to come yet. Now then, Edward – sit down.

EDWARD: I'd like a bit of a wash first.

CHRIS: Martha, old lady, Edward wants a wash.

MARTHA: *(Who is just going out.)* Eh? In your old room, Edward, as usual.

EDWARD: I'll go up then.

MARTHA: Yes. Your soup'll be in by you've got down.

MARTHA goes out and EDWARD is following.

CHRIS: Edward. She's been crying, I see.

EDWARD: Well, a bit. Nothing to speak of.

CHRIS: Been talking of – of her that's gone?

EDWARD: *(Nodding.)* 'm.

CHRIS: Ah. I wanted to tell you one thing, Edward, on that subject, and then never to speak of it agen. By rights you should have been my son-in-law at this moment. You're not, and who's to blame? Why, my daughter – that's gone – to – that's gone. That being so, there's no just cause why you should suffer for another's sin. Me and my wife's comfortably off. After our deaths my property'll go to you, as by right it should have done if you'd married her. That's all.

EDWARD: *(Scratching his head.)* It's very good of you, Mr. Battersby – but – er– well, there's one thing you ought to know –

CHRIS: I want to hear nothing, Edward. I've told you what I'm set on doing, and nothing you can tell me will alter my mind.

EDWARD: Ah! *(He stands thinking, perplexed.)*

Enter MARTHA with a basin of soup.

Well, I suppose I'd better be washing my hands.

He exits quickly.

MARTHA: Why, he's not ready now. Well, it'll keep hot. *(She puts soup on the supper table.)*

What have you been saying to him, Christopher?

CHRIS: Business, Martha, that you wouldn't understand.

MARTHA: Ay.

She sits by the fire. CHRISTOPHER goes to the bureau.

CHRIS: We'll read our chapter when Edward's had his supper. I'll find the place.

He carries a large worn Bible to the oval table in the centre, and places it on the half which is no laid for supper.

Where had we got to?

MARTHA: It's the eighth chapter of St. John tonight.

CHRIS: *(Turning the leaves.)* The eighth chapter of St. John?

MARTHA: Yes. I'm so glad we're in the New Testament again. I wish you wouldn't read the Old, Christopher.

CHRIS: Eh? Why not?

MARTHA: It's not charitable. God was so cruel in the Old Testament. It frightens me.

CHRIS: There was justice done in those days. When a man sinned he was punished. God sent his lightnings and destroyed. There's a deal too much forgiveness about the New Testament. It seems a tempting of Providence to read it to some people.

MARTHA: Don't, Christopher, don't. Surely there's forgiveness for all.

CHRIS: *(Sternly.)* Not for some.

There is a pause. MARTHA sits looking in the fire, and CHRISTOPHER finds the place in the Bible. He is seated behind the table.

Suddenly the door from the hall is quietly opened, and MARY sidles in unheard. She is an attractive-looking, dusky girl, with a rebellious mouth. Her dark hair sweeps down low over her temples. Her dress has been fine once, red and gold predominating in it, but is now shabby. Over it she wears a loose black rain-cloak. A slight wrap is thrown over her head and shoulders. She looks haggard and timid.

After a few seconds CHRISTOPHER feels he is being watched. He turns and sees MARY. He starts and rises slowly, stopping behind the table. They look at each other.

MARY: *(Appealingly.)* Father!

She makes a movement towards him. He puts up his hand and she stops.

MARTHA: *(Hearing the voice and rising.)* Mary! My girl –

CHRIS: Stop where ye are, mother.

MARTHA: Mary, come to me.

She staggers towards MARY. CHRISTOPHER stops her.

CHRIS: Sit ye there.

He places MARTHA in chair on the side of the table away from MARY.

CHRIS. *(To MARY, after a pause)* Well?

MARY: Father!

CHRIS: Ye've come back.

MARY: Yes.

CHRIS: Are ye married?

MARY: *(In a whisper.)* No.

CHRIS: Why not?

MARY: He – he was married already.

CHRIS: When ye went away with him?

MARY: Yes.

CHRIS: And ye knew that?

MARY: Yes.

Pause. CHRISTOPHER bows his head and does not speak.

CHRIS: *(At length.)* What have ye come back for?

MARY: Father!

CHRIS: Why didn't ye stay with him?

MARY: He – he is dead.

CHRIS: Dead! Well?

MARY: So I've – come back.

CHRIS: What for?

MARY: To ask you to let me stay with you.

CHRIS: What right have ye to ask that?

MARTHA: Oh – Father.

CHRIS: *(To MARTHA.)* Tchah!

(To MARY.) Well?

MARY: I'm still your daughter, Father.

CHRIS: Hearken to me – and you, Mother. Three years ago I had a daughter. She was a good girl, I thought. She'd been brought up religious, and we were proud of her.

He pauses and bends his head lower, supporting himself by resting his knuckles on the table before him. He looks down at the table.

But we were wrong. She was bad underneath. Ay, right down wicked all through, in spite of her bringing-up. She'd two good parents, and a young man that was fond of her. But she chose to leave them and go away with a man as she knew couldn't never marry her.

He pauses again.

She made that choice, and must take the consequences. I see no way out of it. Sin must have its punishment. She chose to leave her home, and that done – she leaves it for ever.

MARTHA gives a low cry, and buries her face in her hands on the table. CHRISTOPHER places his hand on her head to comfort her.

CHRIS: Have ye anything to say?

MARY: I wasn't that bad. He promised to marry me when his wife died; she drank, and made his life wretched, I loved him truly – he was very good to me. We've been husband and wife in the sight of Heaven. Then – he died and left me alone.

CHRIS: Had ye any children?

MARY: No.

CHRIS: For that, be thankful.

MARY: I was sorry to leave Edward like I did. But I didn't love him; I didn't know what love was until I met – him. And living here was so dismal, with the chapel hanging over us all the time, and I felt I must make an effort and be free; get away from it all and go with the one I loved.

CHRIS: Ah!

(A pause.)

Have ye anything more to say?

MARY: Only this. The money he left me is all done. I've lived honestly, and I've tried to get work. But I can't. I'm not good at it, and besides, people seem to hesitate about engaging me.

CHRIS: Ah!

MARY: Don't send me away, father. Give me a chance, only one. I've done no wrong perhaps in the sight of Heaven up to now, making his life happier. I've been faithful to him, but – if you send me away now – I don't know what will happen to me. I may become altogether bad.

MARTHA: Father – mercy

CHRIS: She made her choice to leave us three years ago.

MARTHA: Forgive her.

CHRIS: It's not for me to forgive her. She must look higher than me for forgiveness.

MARTHA: But I can forgive her. You don't know how lonely I've been these years, and how I've longed for my child. Mary! *(She rises.)*

CHRIS: Stay where ye are. Don't touch her.

MARY: I see. I understand you, father. I came here to try to live a new life by your help – I knew you were a Christian.

I thought you'd help me. I thought you'd be guided by that Book you have there.

MARTHA: It's the Old Testament he goes by, Mary, the cruel part. I don't; I go by the New, and I forgive you as it tells me to.

CHRIS: Mother, don't speak like that. God knows it's hard for me to do it, but I feel it's so ordered, and I've got to. Not but what there's something in what you says about the New Testament. But I can't rightly decide: I'm not a fit judge. I'm too – too broad minded. As a religious man I feel she's accursed, and as a father I'm casting about for an excuse to pardon her. But I can't rightly find it. I think he as should have been your husband has a right to speak in this.

MARY: Edward! Is he here? I can't face him.

EDWARD enters briskly, and seeing MARY stops dead. MARY sinks in chair by the door and hides her face.

MARTHA: *(Feverishly.)* Edward, Edward, Mary's come back as I've prayed. Father does not know what to do; he thinks he ought to send her away, but I'm begging him to forgive her. He can't tell what to do. Father, Edward will decide. Edward has always promised me to marry her if she came back. He can forgive her – Edward'll marry her, father. Will you be guided by him? You don't rightly know what to do, you say. Let him decide. Father! Father! Let Edward decide.

She sinks on her knees before CHRISTOPHER.

CHRIS: Edward has always promised to marry her! Have ye promised my wife that?

EDWARD: *(Helplessly.)* Yes – yes – I have.

MARTHA: Yes – he has, always. Edward's not so fond of the chapel; but he's a better man than you, father.

CHRIS: Then I see my way clear. The judgment's taken out of my hands. It's in Edward's. If he'll marry this girl notwithstanding her sin, then I take it as a sign that she may be forgiven. If not – she goes for ever from beneath my roof.

MARTHA: Mary, my girl, you're saved! He's told me many a time he'd marry you.

CHRIS: Be silent, Martha. I don't ask my daughter's consent. That she'll give, I take it, without question.

He looks at her; she does not raise her head. CHRISTOPHER turns to EDWARD.

It's for you to say.

EDWARD: You're not leaving it to me, are you?

CHRIS: Yes.

EDWARD: But I'd rather you didn't. Don't put it like that. Forgive the girl, Mr. Battersby, and then we'll see.

CHRIS: It's for you to decide.

A pause. EDWARD stands half-dazed.

MARTHA: Edward!

CHRIS: Martha! Well, my lad?

EDWARD does not reply; he scratches his head.

CHRIS: Ah, I take it ye won't.

EDWARD: Oh, it's not good enough putting it like this.

CHRIS: Ye won't?

EDWARD: I can't – I can't.

MARTHA: Ah!

She gives a despairing cry. CHRISTOPHER, who has been anxiously awaiting EDWARD's decision, sways and nearly breaks down. He regains control of himself.

CHRIS: Ah! He can't marry her. I don't ask reasons.

EDWARD: But I must – I must tell you why.

MARTHA: Oh! And he always promised me!

EDWARD: I know I did, and I meant it at first. But as time went on, I thought less of her, you see – Mary, I mean – and – and –

MARTHA: But he always promised me.

EDWARD: Ay, I did. I kept on promising you. I hadn't the heart to tell you I'd changed. Every time I came you asked me, and I couldn't bear to tell you no; for I never thought Mary would come back.

CHRIS: Edward, think once again. It's because she is what she is that you can't marry her?

EDWARD: No. It's because I was married to a girl in Nottingham last week.

MARTHA: Ah, and he promised me.

EDWARD: You'll not be guided by me, Mr. Battersby? I couldn't be expected to wait for ever.

CHRIS: Edward, I don't blame you. You'd a right to do as you thought best. That finishes it. With what happens now, you've nothing to do.

EDWARD: I – I'd best go, I think.

CHRIS: I think so.

EDWARD: *(Takes his coat from the chair by the fire.)* I'm sorry about this.

He crosses to the door, and stops in front of MARY. She does not look at him. He opens the door.

Well! Good night, all.

CHRIS: Edward I'd like to tell you that this will make no difference to my will. It'll all go to you.

EDWARD: I'd a good deal rather you left it to – to her.

CHRIS: Good night, Edward.

EDWARD goes out and shuts the door. Shortly afterwards the outer door closes. There is a long pause.

MARTHA· *(In a whisper.)* He always promised me.

CHRIS: That's enough, mother.

He turns and looks at MARY.

MARY: I'm to go?

CHRISTOPHER bows his head.

Very well, I'll go. I came here repenting and wanting to be saved. I might have known you better. Mother's right when she says you go by the Old Testament. Much good your religion will do you now. I don't envy you when you go to the chapel on Sunday and kneel and say, 'Forgive us our trespasses'. You must learn to forgive other people's before you ask for your own to be forgiven.

CHRIS: The judgment was taken out of my hands.

MARY: Yes, I'll go. And what to do? I don't care. I'll not work; I'm not made for it. Why should I try and be good when I see what sort of people religion makes? I've enough money to take me back to London – to the London streets.

CHRIS: You're going to damnation?

MARY: And if I am, it's you as has sent me there.

CHRIS: *(Tonelessly.)* The judgment was taken out of my hands.

MARY: Good-bye, mother.

MARTHA: *(Rising.)* Mary – my girl – Come back.

MARY opens the door.

MARTHA: Oh, I've been so lonely. I want to kiss my girl before she goes.

She moves towards MARY.

CHRIS: Keep back!

MARY: I've a right to kiss her good-bye.

CHRIS: You shan't touch her. She is pure.

MARTHA: Mary! Mary!

CHRISTOPHER helps her to a chair by fire.

MARY: Good-bye, dear mother.

She waves a kiss to MARTHA. MARY goes out and closes the door. CHRISTOPHER goes to table and sits. MARTHA has fainted in her chair.

CHRIS: *(With intense agony.)* My child – my dear child!

He bows his head on his arms. The outer door closes.

(Raising his head and controlling himself.) We'll just read that chapter together, mother, before we go to rest. The eighth chapter of St. John's Gospel.

LONESOME-LIKE
BY HAROLD BRIGHOUSE

The interior of a cottage in a Lancashire village. Through the window at the back the grey row of cottages opposite is just visible. The outside door is next to the window. Door L. As regards furniture the room is very bare. For example, there are several square patches where the distemper of the walls is of a darker shade than the rest, indicating the places once occupied by pictures. There is an uncovered deal table and two chairs by it near the fireplace R. Attached to the L wall is a dresser and a place-rack above it containing a few pots. The dresser has also one or two utensils upon it. A blackened kettle rests on the top of the cooking range, but the room contains only the barest necessities. The floor is uncarpeted, but a yard of cheap muslin is fastened across the window, not coming, however, high enough to prevent a passer-by from looking in should he wish to do so. On the floor, near the fire, is a battered black tin trunk, the lid of which is raised. On a peg behind the door L is a black silk skirt and bodice and an old-fashioned beaded bonnet. The time is afternoon.

As the curtain rises the room is empty. Immediately, however, the door L opens and SARAH ORMEROD, an old woman, enters carrying clumsily in her arms a couple of pink flannelette nightdresses, folded neatly. Her black stuff dress is well worn, and her wedding-ring is her only ornament. She wears elastic-sided boots, and her rather short skirt shows a pair of grey worsted stockings. SARAH crosses and puts the nightdresses on the table, surveying the trunk ruefully. There is a knock at the outside door and she looks up.

SARAH: Who's theer?

EMMA: *(Off.)* It's me, Mrs Ormerod, Emma Brierley.

SARAH: Eh, coom in, Emma, lass.

EMMA BRIERLEY enters. She is a young weaver, and, having just left her work, she wears a dark shirt, a blouse of some indeterminate blue-grey shade made of cotton, and a large shawl over her head and shoulders in place of a jacket and hat. A coloured cotton apron covers her skirt below the waist, and the short skirt displays stout stockings similar to Sarah's. She wears clogs, and the clothes – except the shawl – are covered with ends of cotton and cotton wool fluff. Even her hair has not escaped. A pair of scissors hangs by a cord from her waist.

Tha's kindly welcoom. It's good o' thee to think o' coomin' to see an ould woman like me.

EMMA: *(By the door.)* Nought o' th' sort, Mrs Ormerod. Th' mill's just loosed and A thowt A'd step in as A were passin' and see 'ow tha was feeling like.

SARAH: *(Crossing to the box.)* Oh, nicely, nicely, thankee. It's only my 'ands as is gone para lytic, tha knaws, an' a weaver's no manner o' good to nobody without th' use o' 'er 'ands. A'm all reeght in masel'. That's worst of it.

EMMA: Well, while A'm 'ere, Mrs Ormerod, is theer nought as A can do for thee?

SARAH: A dunno as theer is, thankee, Emma.

EMMA: *(Taking her shawl off, looking round and hanging it on a peg at the door.)* Well, A knaws better. What wert doin' when A coom in? Packin' yon box?

SARAH: Aye. Tha sees theer's a two three things as A canna bear thowt o' parting from. A don't reeghtly knaw if they'll let me tak' 'em into the workus wi' me, but A canna have 'em sold we' rest of stuff.

EMMA: *(Crossing below SARAH to the box, and going on her knees.)* Let me help yo.

SARAH: Tha's a good lass, Emma. A'd tak' it kindly of thee.

EMMA: They'd do wi' packin' a bit closer. A dunno as they'd carry safe that road.

SARAH: A know. It's my 'ands tha sees, as mak's it difficult for me. *(She sits on a chair LC.)*

EMMA: *(Burying her arms in the box and rearranging its contents.)* Aye. A'll soon settle 'em a bit tighter.

SARAH: But what's 'appened to thy looms, lass? They'll not weave by 'emselves while thee's 'ere, tha knows.

EMMA: *(Looking round.)* Eh, looms is all reeght. Factory's stopped. It's Saturday afternoon.

SARAH: So 'tis. A'd clean forgot. A do forget time o' th' week sittin' 'ere day arter day wi' nought to do.

EMMA: *(Resuming at the box.)* So that's all reeght. Tha's no need to worry about me. Tha's got trouble enough of thy own.

SARAH: Aye, th'art reeght theer, lass. Theer's none on us likes to think o' going to workus when we're ould.

EMMA: 'Appen it'll be all reeght after all. Parson's coomin' to see thee.

SARAH: Aye, A knaw 'e is. A dunno, but A'm in 'opes 'e'll do summat for me. Tha can't never tell what them folks can do.

EMMA: *(Kneeling up.)* Tha keep thy pecker oop, Mrs Ormerod. That's what my moother says to me when A tould 'er A were coomin' in to thee. Keep 'er pecker oop, she says. It's not as if she'd been lazy or a wastrel, she says; Sal Ormerod's bin a 'ard worker in 'er day, she says. It's not as if it were thy fault. Tha can't 'elp tha 'ands going paralytic. *(She continues rummaging in the box while speaking.)*

SARAH: Naw. It's not my fault. God knaws A'm game enough for work, ould as A am. A allays knawed as A'd 'ave to work for my living all th' days o' my life. A never was a savin' sort.

EMMA: Theer's nowt against thee for that. Theer's some as can be careful o' theer brass an' some as can't. It's not a virtue, it's a gift. That's what my moother allays says. *(She resumes packing.)*

SARAH: She's reeght an' all. We never 'ad the gift o' savin', my man and me. An' when Tom Ormerod took an' died, the club money as A drew all went on 'is funeral an' 'is gravestone. A warn't goin' to 'ave it said as 'e warn't buried proper.

EMMA: It were a beautiful funeral, Mrs Ormerod.

SARAH: Aye.

EMMA: A will say that, beautiful it were. A never seen a better, an' A goes to all as A can. *(She rises.)* A dotes on buryin's. Are these the next? *(She crosses C to the table, takes the nightdresses, and resumes packing.)*

SARAH: Aye.

EMMA puts them in and rests on her knees listening to SARAH's next speech.

(After a pause.)

A've been a 'ouseproud woman all my life, Emma, an A've took pride in 'aving my bits o' sticks as good as another's. Even th' manager's missus oop to factory 'ouse theer, she never 'ad a better show 'o furniture nor me, though A says it as shouldn't. An' it tak's brass to keep a decent 'ouse over your yead. An' we allays' ad our full week's 'ollydayin' at Blackpool reg'lar at Wakes time. Us didn't'ave no childer o' our own to spend it on, an' us spent it on ourselves. A allays 'ad a plenty o' good food in th' 'ouse an' never stinted nobody, an' Tom 'e liked 'is beer an' 'is baccy. 'E were a pigeon-fancier too in 'is day, were my Tom, an' pigeon-fancying runs away wi' a mint o' money. No. Soom'ow theer never was no brass to put in th' Savings bank. We was allays spent oop coom wages neeght.

EMMA: A knaw, Mrs Ormerod. May be A'm young, but A knaw 'ow 'tis. We works cruel 'ard in th' mill, an', when us plays, us plays as 'ard too, *(Pause.)* an' small blame to us either. It's out *own* we're spendin'.

SARAH: Aye. It's a 'ard life, the factory 'and's. A can mind me many an' many's the time when th' warnin' bell went on th' factory lodge at ha'f past five of a winter's mornin' as A've craved for another ha'f hour in my bed, but Tom 'e got me oop an' we was never after six passin' through them factory gates all th' years we were wed. There's not many as can say they were never late. 'Work or Clem,' that were what Tom allays tould me th' ould bell were sayin'. An 'e were reeght, Emma, 'Work or Clem' is God's truth.

(EMMA's head is in the box.)

An' now th' time's coom when A can't work no more. But Parson's a good man, e'll mak' it all reeght.

(EMMA's head appears.)

Eh, it were good o' thee to coom in, lass. A bit o' coompany do mak' a world o' difference. Ah'm twice as cheerful as A were.

EMMA: A'm glad to 'ear tha say so, Mrs Ormerod. *(She rises from the box.)* Is theer owt else?

SARAH: A were thinking A'd like to tak' my black silk as A've worn o' Sundays this many a year, but A canna think its reeght thing for workus.

EMMA: Oh, thee tak' it, Mrs Ormerod.

SARAH: A'd dearly love to. Tha sees A'm noan in debt, nobbut what chairs an table 'ull pay for, and A doan't like thowt o' leaving owt as A'm greatly fond of.

EMMA: Yo doan't Mrs Ormerod. Thee tak' it. Wheer is it? A'll put un in. Theer's lots o' room on top. A'll see un's noan crushed.

SARAH: It's hanging theer behind door.

EMMA crosses back to the door, and gets the clothes.

A got un out to show Parson. A thowt A'd ask un if it were proper to tak' it if A've to go. My best bonnet's with it, an 'all.

EMMA goes below the table, takes the frock, folds it on the table and packs it.

EMMA: I'll put un in.

SARAH: A'm being a lot 'o trouble to thee, lass.

EMMA: That's nowt, neighbours mun be neighbourly. *(She gets the bonnet from the table and packs it.)*

SARAH: *(Pausing and looking round.)* Place doan't look much an' that's a fact. Th' furniture's bin goin' bit by bit, and theer's nought much left to part wi' now.

EMMA: Never mind, it 'ull be all reeght now Parson's takken thee oop.

SARAH: A'm hopin' so. A *am* hopin' so. A never could abide th' thowt o' th' workus – me as 'as bin an 'ard workin' woman. A couldn't fancy sleepin' in a strange bed wi' strange folk round me, an' when th' workus master said 'Do that' A'd 'ave to do it, an' when he said 'Go theer' A'd 'ave to a' gone wheer he tould me – me as 'as allays 'eld my yead 'igh an' gone the way A pleased masel'. Eh, it's a terrible thowt, the workus.

EMMA: *(Rising.)* Now tha's sure that's all?

SARAH: *(Pausing and considering.)* Eh, if A havna forgot my neeghtcaps. *(Rising, moving C and stopping.)* A suppose they'll let me wear un in yonder. A doan't reeghtly think as A'd get my rest proper wi'out my neeghtcaps.

EMMA: Oh, they'll let thee wear un all reeght.

SARAH: *(As she goes.)* A'll go an' get un.

SARAH goes out R and returns presently with the white nightcaps.

That's all now.

SARAH gives them to EMMA, who meets her C.

EMMA: *(Putting them in.)* Yo never 'ad no childer, did yo, Mrs Ormerod?

SARAH: No, Emma, no – may be that's as broad as 's long.

She sits above the fire.

Yo never knaw 'ow they go. Soom on 'em turn again yo when they're growed or they get wed themselves an' forget all as yo've done for 'em, like a many A could name, and they're allays a worrit to yo when they're young.

EMMA: A meeght be testing that before so long wi' childer o' ma own. A'll chance their being a burden to me.

SARAH: Nay, Emma! A bit lass like yo' wi' childer!

EMMA: A'm getting wed soon, Mrs Ormerod.

SARAH: Getting wed! Think o'that! Why, it seems t'were nobbut t'other day as tha' went running about in short frocks, an' now tha's growd up and gettin' thasel' wed. Time do run on. Well, tha's not one of them graceless good-for-nowts. Tha'll never forget thy moother, A knaw, nor what she's done for thee. Who's tha keepin' coompany with?

EMMA: It's Joe Hindle as goes wi' me, Mrs Ormerod.

SARAH: 'Indle, 'Indle? What, not son to Robert 'Indle, 'im as used to be overlooker in th' factory till 'e went to foreign parts to learn them Roossioans 'ow to weave?

EMMA: Aye, that's 'im.

SARAH: Well, A dunno ought about th' lad. 'Is faither were a fine man. A minds 'im well. But A'll tell this, Emma, an' A'll tell it thee to they faice, 'e's doin' well for 'isself is young Joe 'Indle.

EMMA: Thankee, Mrs Ormerod.

SARAH: Sithee, Emma, tha's a good lass. A've gotten an ould teapot in yonder *(Indicating her bedroom.)* as my mother give me when A was wed. A weren't for packing it in box because o' risk o' breaking it. A were going to carry in in my arms. A'd a mind to keep it till A died, but A reckon A'll 'ave no use for it in workus.

EMMA: Tha's not gone theer yet.

SARAH: Never mind that. *(She slowly rises.)* A'm going to give it thee, lass, for a weddin'-gift. Tha'll tak' care of it, A knaw, and when thy eye catches it, 'appen tha'll spare me a thowt.

EMMA: Oh no, Mrs Ormerod, A couldn't think o' takkin' it.

SARAH: Art too proud to tak' a gift from me?

EMMA: No. Tha knaws A'm not.

SARAH: Then hold thy hush. A'll be back in a minute. Happen A'd best tidy masel' up too against Parson cooms.

EMMA: Can A help thee, Mrs Ormerod?

SARAH: No, lass, no. A can do a bit for masel'. My 'ands isn't that bad, A canna weave wi' 'em, but A can do all as A need to.

EMMA: Well, A'll do box up. *(She crosses to the table R and gets the cord.)*

SARAH: Aye.

EMMA: All reeght.

SARAH exits. A man's face appears outside at the window. He surveys the room, and then the face vanishes as he knocks at the door.

Who's theer?

SAM: *(Off.)* It's me, Sam Horrocks.

EMMA crosses L and opens the door.

May A coom in?

EMMA: What dost want?

SAM: *(On the doorstep.)* A want a word wi' thee, Emma Brierley. A followed thee oop from factory and A've bin waitin' out theer till A'm tired o' waitin'.

EMMA: Well, tha'd better coom in. A 'avent't time to talk wi' thee at door.

EMMA lets him in, closes the door, and, leaving him standing in the middle of the room, resumes work on her knees at the box. SAM HORROCKS is a hulking young man of a rather vacant expression. He is dressed in mechanic's blue dungarees. His face is oily and his clothes stained. He wears boots, not clogs. He mechanically takes a ball of oily black cotton-waste from his right pocket when in conversational difficulties and wipes his hands upon it. He has a red muffler round his neck without collar, and his shock of fair hair is surmounted by a greasy black cap, which covers perhaps one tenth of it.

SAM: *(After watching EMMA's back for a moment.)* Wheer's Mrs Ormerod?

EMMA: *(Without looking up.)* What's that to do wi' thee?

SAM: *(Apologetically.)* A were only askin'. Tha needn't be short wi' a chap.

EMMA: She's in scullery washin' 'er if tha wants to knaw.

SAM: Oh!

EMMA: *(Looking at him over her shoulder after a slight pause.)* Doan't tha tak' they cap off in 'ouse, Sam Horrock?

SAM: Naw.

EMMA: Well, tha can tak' it off in this 'ouse or get t' other side o' door.

SAM: *(Taking off his cap and stuffing it in his left pocket after trying his right and finding the ball of waste in it.)* Yes, Emma. A kna' A'm outrageous bold comin' in 'ere like this. But A'm that wrought up tha' wouldn't believe.

EMMA resumes work with her back towards him and waits for him to speak. But he is not ready yet.

EMMA: Well, what dost want?

SAM: Nought... Eh, but tha art a gradely wench.

EMMA: What's that to do wi' thee?

SAM: Nought.

EMMA: Then just tha mind thy own business, an' doan't pass compliments behind folks' backs.

SAM: A didn't mean no 'arm.

EMMA: Well?

SAM: It's a fine day, isn't it? For th' time o' th' year?

EMMA: Aye.

SAM: A very fine day.

EMMA: Aye.

SAM: *(Desperately.)* It's a damned fine day.

EMMA: Aye.

SAM: *(After a moment.)* Dost know my 'ouse, Emma?

EMMA: Aye.

SAM: Wert ever in it?

EMMA: Not sin' tha moother died.

SAM: Naw. A suppose not. Not sin' ma moother died. She were a fine woman, ma moother, for all she were bedridden.

EMMA: She were better than 'er son, though that's not saying much neither.

SAM: Naw, but tha does mind ma 'ouse, Emma, as it were when she were alive.

EMMA: Aye.

SAM: A've done a bit at it sin' them days. Got a new quilt on bed from Co-op. Red un it is wi' blue stripes down 'er.

EMMA: Aye.

SAM: Well, Emma?

EMMA: *(Over her shoulder.)* Well, what? What's thy 'ouse an' thy quilt to do wi' me?

SAM: Oh nought… Tha doesn't 'elp a feller much, neither.

EMMA rises and faces him. SAM is behind the corner table and backs a little before her.

EMMA: What's tha gettin' at, Sam Horrocks? Tha's got a tongue in thy faice, hasn't tha?

SAM: A suppose so. A doan't use it much though.

EMMA: No. Tha's not much better than a tongue-tied idiot, Sam Horrocks, allays mooning about in th' engine-house in day-time an' sulkin' at 'ome neeght-time.

SAM: Aye, A'm lonely sin' ma moother died. She did 'ave a way wi' 'er, ma moother.

EMMA: She'd a rough-tongued way from what A've 'eard tell of it.

SAM: She 'ad an' all. She were a masterpiece of scolding. Tha'd scarce credit the gift she 'ad for chiding. It fell like an 'ail-storm from 'er little body. Th' ould plaice as none been same to me sin' she died. It's that unnatural quiet. Day-time, tha knaws, A'm all reeght. Tha sees, them engines, them an' me's pals. They talks to me an' A understands their ways. A doan't some'ow seem to understand the ways o' folks like as A does th' ways o' them engines.

EMMA: Tha doesn't try. T'other lads goes rattin' or dog-feeghtin' on a Sunday or to a football match of a Saturday afternoon. Tha stays moonin' about th' 'ouse. Tha's not likely to understand folks. Tha's not sociable.

SAM: Naw. That's reeght enough. A nobbut get laughed at when A tries to be sociable an' stand my corner down at th' pub wi' th' rest o' th' lads. It's no use ma tryin' to soop ale, A can't carry th' drink like t'others. A knaws A've ways o' ma own.

EMMA: Tha has that.

SAM: A'm terrible lonesome, Emma. That theer 'ouse o' mine, it do want a wench about th' plaice. Th' engines is all reeght for days, but th' neeghts is that lonesome-like tha wouldn't believe.

EMMA: Tha's only thasel' to blame. It's nought to do wi' me, choosehow.

SAM: Naw? A'd – A'd 'oped as 'ow it might 'ave, Emma.

EMMA: *(Approaching threateningly.)* Sam Horrocks, if tha doan't tell me proper what tha means A'll give tha such a slap in the mouth.

SAM: *(Backing before her.)* Tha does fluster a feller, Emma. Just like ma moother.

EMMA: A wish A 'ad bin. A'd 'ave knocked some sense into thy silly yead.

SAM: *(Suddenly and clumsily kneeling above the chair L of the table.)* Wilt tha 'ave me, Emma? A mak' good money in th' engine-house.

EMMA: Get oop, tha great fool. If tha didn't keep thasel' so close wi' tha moonin' about in th' engine-'ouse an' never speakin' a word to nobody tha'd knaw A were keepin' coompany wi' Joe Hindle.

SAM: *(Scrambling up.)* Is that a fact, Emma?

EMMA: Of course it's a fact. Bann's 'ull be oop come Sunday fortneeght. We've not 'idden it neither. It's just like the great blind idiot that tha art not to 'a' seen it long enough sin'.

SAM: A wern't aware. By gum, A 'ad so 'oped as tha'd 'ave me, Emma.

EMMA: *(A little more softly.)* A'm sorry if A've 'urt thee, Sam.

SAM: Aye. It were ma fault. Eh, well, A think mebbe A'd best be goin'.

EMMA: *(Lifting the box to L.)* Aye. Parson's coomin' to see Mrs Ormerod in a minute.

SAM: *(With pride.)* A knaw all about that, anyhow.

EMMA: She'm in a bad way. A dunno masel' as Parson can do much for 'er.

SAM: A've 'eard of cases. It's wunnerful what them powerful men can do.

EMMA: Tha's 'eard of cases when th' ould folk could still work. Only she'd beyond doing much for 'ersel', leave alone scrubbing floors for others. A tell thee, Sam, A mis doubt Parson. If she's bin pestering 'im, e's as like…

SAM: Nay, she'd never do that.

EMMA: She pestered weaving manager, didn't she?

SAM: A dunno.

EMMA: Well, she did. Asked him if she 'adn't earned a pension. 'E laughed at 'er.

SAM: Parson didn't laugh, seemingly.

EMMA: Like as not 'e said summat comforting to get shut of 'er an' gave more 'ope than 'e meant.

SAM: A'm the hopeful sort masel'.

EMMA: Tha' art that. Cherishing 'opes of me.

SAM: Aye, well, A'm grieved for that. A meant no offence, Emma. A'd 'ave asked thee first if A'd known 'e were after thee. A've bin trying long enough only A rarely saw thee by thasel' an' when A did words wouldn't come to fit the bigness o' ma feelings. A allays were backward but A did a lot of looking. Tha mebbe saw me looking – mebbe?

EMMA: A didn't notice in particular.

SAM looks hurt.

There's a many looked at me.

SAM: That's for certain sure. An' if so be as my looking weren't noted it didna give offence.

EMMA: *(Touching his arm.)* Nay, luv, there's no offence. Tha's a good lad if tha art a fool an' mebbe tha's not to blame for that. Good-bye.

SAM: Good-bye, Emma. An'… An' A 'ope 'e'll mak' thee 'appy. A'd dearly like to coom to th' weddin' an' shake 'is 'and.

MRS ORMEROD is heard off L.

EMMA: A'll see tha's asked. Theer's Mrs Ormerod stirrin' now. Tha'd best be gettin'.

SAM: All reeght. Good-bye, Emma.

EMMA: Good-bye, Sam.

SAM exits LC. MRS ORMEROD comes from the inside door. She has a small blue teapot in her hand.

SARAH: Was anybody 'ere, Emma? A thowt A yeard someun talkin', only my yearin' isn't what it used to be, an' A warn't sure.

EMMA: It were Sam Horrocks, Mrs Ormerod.

SARAH: Yon lad of ould Sal Horrocks as died last year? 'Im as isn't reeght in 'is yead?

EMMA: Aye. 'E's bin askin' me to wed 'im.

SARAH: *(Incensed.)* In my 'ouse? Theer's imperence for thee, an' tha promised to another lad, an' all. A'd 'ave set about 'im wi' a stick, Emma.

EMMA: 'E didn't knaw about Joe. It made me feel cruel like to 'ave to tell 'im.

SARAH: 'E'll get ower it. Soom lass'll tak' 'im, marred as 'e is.

EMMA: A suppose so.

SARAH: *(Coming down, putting the teapot in EMMA's hands.)* Well, theer's teapot.

EMMA: *(Meeting SARAH RC; examining the teapot.)* It's beautiful. Beautiful, it is, Mrs Ormerod.

SARAH: Aye, it's a bit o' real china is that. Tha'll tak' care on't, lass, won't thee?

EMMA: A will an' all.

SARAH: Aye. A knaw it's safe wi' thee. Mebbe safer than it would be in workus. A can't think well on yon plaice. A goa cold all ower at thowt of it.

There is a knock at the door.

EMMA: That'll be Parson.

SARAH: *(Crossing L; smoothing her hair.)* Goa an' look through window first, an' see who 'tis.

EMMA: *(Putting the teapot on the table; looking through the window.)* It's not the ould Parson. It's one o' them young curate chaps.

SARAH: Well, coom away from window an' sit thee down. It won't do to seem too eager. Let un knock again if it's not th' ould Parson.

EMMA leaves the window and goes R of the table. The knock is repeated.

(Raising her voice.) Coom in so who tha art. Door's on latch.

The Rev. FRANK ALLEYNE enters. He is a young curate, a Londoner and an Oxford man, by association, training, and taste, totally unfitted for a Lancashire curacy, in which he is unfortunately no exception.

FRANK: Good afternoon, Mrs Ormerod.

SARAH: Good day to thee.

FRANK: I'm sorry to say Mr Blundell had had to go to a missionary meeting, but asked me to come and see you in his stead.

SARAH: Tha's welcom, lad. Sit thee down.

EMMA comes below the table L. She dusts a chair L of the table, which doesn't need it, with her apron. ALLEYNE raises a deprecatory hand. SARAH's familiarity, as it seems to him, offends him. He looks sourly at EMMA and markedly ignores her.

FRANK: Thank you; no, I won't sit, I cannot stay long.

SARAH: Just as tha likes. It's all same to me.

EMMA stays by R of the table.

FRANK: How is it with you, Mrs Ormerod?

SARAH: It might be worse. A've lost th' use o' my 'ands, and they're takkin' me to workus, but A'm not dead yet, and that's summat to be thankful for.

FRANK: Oh yes, yes, Mrs Ormerod. The – er – message I am to deliver is, I fear, not quite what Mr Blundell led you to hope for. His efforts on your behalf have – er – unfortunately failed. He finds himself obliged to give up all hope of aiding you to a livelihood. In fact – er – I understand that the arrangements made for your removal to the workhouse this afternoon must be carried out. It seems there is no alternative. I am grieved to be the bearer of bad tidings, but I am sure you will find a comfortable home awaiting you, Mrs – er – Ormerod.

SARAH: 'Appen A shall an' 'appen A shan't. Theer's no tellin' 'ow you'll favour a thing till you've tried it.

FRANK: You must resign yourself to the will of providence. The consolations of religion are always with us. Shall I pray with you?

SARAH: A never were much for prayin' when A were well off, an' A doubt the Lord ud tak' it kind o' selfish o' me if A coom cryin' to 'im now A'm 'urt.

FRANK: He will understand. Can I do nothing for you?

SARAH: A dunno as tha can, thankin' thee all same.

FRANK: I am privileged with Mr Blundell's permission to bring a little gift to you, Mrs Ormerod. *(Feeling in his coat tails and bringing out a Testament.)* Allow me to present you with this Testament, and may it help you to bear your Cross with resignation.

He hands her the Testament. SARAH does not raise her hands, and it drops on her lap. ALLEYNE takes it again and puts it on the table.

Ah, yes, of course – your poor hands… I understand.

SARAH: Thankee kindly. Readin' don't coom easy to me, an' my eyes aren't what they were, but A'll mak' most of it.

FRANK: You will never read that in vain. And now, dear sister, I must go. I will pray for strength for you. All will be will. Good day.

SARAH: Good day to thee.

ALLEYNE exits.

EMMA: Tha doesn't look so pleased wi' tha gift, Mrs Ormerod.

SARAH: It's not square thing of th' ould Parson, Emma. 'E should a coom an' tould me 'isself. Looks like 'e were feart to do it. A never could abide them curate lads. We doan't want no grand Lunnon gentlemen down 'ere. 'E doan't understand us no more than we understand 'im. 'E means all reeght, poor lad. Sithee, Emma, A've bin a Churchgoin' woman all my days. A was browt oop to Church, an' many's th' bit o' brass they've 'ad out o' me in my time. An' in th' end they send me a fine curate with a tuppenny Testament. That's all th' good yo get out o' they folks.

EMMA: We'm chapel in our 'ouse, an' 'e didn't forget to let me see 'e knaw'd it, but A doan't say as it's ony different wi' chapels, neither. They get what they can outer yo, but yo mustn't look for nothin' back, when th' pinch cooms.

SARAH: Nay, now, Emma, we're both saying things we don't mean. We'll none lose hold o' our proper respect. Come to it, yon feller's 'elped me. A'm getting th' picture o' masel as others see me.

EMMA: What picture's that?

SARAH: An' ould woman too far gone to knit a stocking. Neither Parson not nobody else can 'elp me to 'elp ma 'elpless self. Nobody, barring workus master. It's the reeght plaice for the likes o' me. Doing what workus master bids me.

EMMA: An' he'd best watch out an' all. If yon man don't treat thee gentle 'e'll meet me on a dark neeght wi' a clog in ma 'and.

SARAH: Eh, lass, tha's full o' Christian kindness.

EMMA: It's all A am full of, an' all.

A clock strikes three o'clock in the distance.

There's Town Hall going three. Ma dinner's waited above a bit.

SARAH: Eh, what's that, lass? Dost mean to tell me tha's bin clemmin' all this time?

EMMA: A coom 'ere straight from factory.

SARAH: An' A've nought to offer thee. Sarah Ormerod wi' a guest in her house an' th' cupboard bare.

EMMA: My dinner's ready for me at whoam, Mrs Ormerod.

SARAH: Then just look sharp an' get it, tha silly lass. Tha's no reeght to go wi'out thy baggin'.

EMMA: *(Putting her shawl on.)* All reeght. A'm off.

She picks up the teapot.

SARAH: Tha's bin a world o' comfort to me, Emma. It'll be
'arder to bear when tha's gone. Th' thowt's too much for
me. Eh, lass, A'm feart o' yon great gaunt building wi' th'
drear windows.

EMMA: 'Appen ma moother 'ull coom in. Tha'll do wi' a bit o'
coompany. A'll ask her to coom an' fetch thee a coop o' tea
by an' bye.

There is a knock at the door.

SARAH: Who's theer?

SAM: *(Off.)* It's only me, Mrs Ormerod.

EMMA: A do declare it's that Sam Horrocks again.

SARAH: Sam Horrocks! What can th' lad be after now?
(Calling.) Hast tha wiped thy boots on scraper?

SAM: Yes, Mrs Ormerod.

SARAH: Coom in then.

SAM enters.

Tak' thy cap off.

SAM: Yes, Mrs Ormerod.

SARAH: What dost want?

SAM: A've soom business 'ere. A thowt A'd find thee by thysel'.
A'll coom again. *(He bolts nervously for the door.)*

SARAH: Let that door be. Doest say tha's got business 'ere?

SAM: Aye, wi' thee. A'd like a word wi' thee private.

EMMA moves to the open door.

SARAH: All reeght. Emma's just goin' to 'er dinner.

EMMA: *(Speaking through the door.)* A'll ask my moother to step in later on, Mrs Ormerod, and thank thee very much for th' teapot.

SARAH: A'll be thankful if she'll coom.

EMMA exits with the teapot.

Now Sam Horrocks, what's the matter wi' thee?

SAM: *(Dropping the cotton waste he is fumbling him and picking it up.)* It's fine day for th' time o' th' year.

SARAH: Didst want to see me private to tell me that, lad?

SAM: Naw, not exactly.

SARAH: Well, what is it then? Coom, lad, A'm waitin' on thee. Art tongue-tied? Can't tha quit mawlin' yon bit o' waste an' tell me what 'tis tha wants?

SAM: *(Desperately.)* Mebbe it'll not be so fine in th' mornin'. Sunday, tha' knows. It often rains on a Sunday.

SARAH: A'll tell thee what A'd do to thee if A 'ad the use o' my 'ands, my lad. A'd coom aside thee and A'd box thy ears. If tha's got business wi' me, tha'd best state it sharp or A'll be showin' thee the shape o' my door.

SAM: Tha do fluster a feller so as A doan't knaw wheer A am. A've not been nagged like that theer sin' my ould moother died.

SARAH: A've 'eerd folk say Sal Horrocks were a slick un wi' 'er tongue.

SAM: *(Admiringly.)* She were that. Rare talker she were. She'd lie theer in 'er bed all day as it might be in yon corner, an' call me all th' names she could put her tongue to, till A couldn't tell ma reeght 'and from ma left. *(Still reminiscent.)* Wonnerful spirit, she 'ad, considerin' she were bed-ridden so long. Tha'd expect she'd sometimes 'ave to stop for breath. Stopped for bobbins, like in weaving shed. But not

84

'er, not ma moother when the fancy took 'er to mention all she thowt about me.

SARAH: That 'ud tak' time all reeght, if she nobbut mentioned 'alf o' th' whole.

SAM: She never wearied. A tell thee, Mrs Ormerod, them engines at mill 'ave sweetest diive of any machine in Lancashire. A've the biggest dam' respect in th' world for them engines, aye, but job for job, their drive against th' drive o' ma moother's tongue, A'd back ma moother every time. She'd a terrible knowledge of burning words, being a great reader of the Bible. She were only a little un an' a cripple an' all, but by gum she could sling it at a feller if 'er tea weren't brewed to 'er taste. Talk! She'd talk a donkey's yead off, she would.

SARAH: *(On her mettle.)* An' A'll talk thy silly yead off an' all if tha doan't get sharp to tellin' me what tha wants after in my 'ouse, tha great mazed idiot.

SAM: Eh, but she were a rare un.

SARAH: The lad's daft aboot his moother.

SAM: *(After a pause; detachedly, looking at the window.)* Wunnerful breeght the sky is to day.

SARAH: Tha great 'ulkin fool. A'd tak' a broomstick to thee if – if A'd the use o' my 'ands.

SAM: Now, if that isn't just what ma moother used to say.

SARAH: Dang thy moother. An' A doan't mean no disrespect to 'er neither. She's bin in 'er grave this year an' more, poor woman.

SAM: A can 'elp thinkin' to 'er all same. Eh, but she were wunnerful.

SARAH: An' A'd be wunnerful too. A'd talk to thee. A'd call thee if A were thy moother an' A'd to live aside 'o thee neeght an' day.

SAM: *(Eagerly.)* Eh, by gum, but A wish tha would.

SARAH: Would what?

SAM: Would coom an' live along wi' me.

SARAH: Tha great fool, what dost mean? Art askin' me to wed thee?

SAM: A didn't mean to offend thee, Mrs Ormerod. A'm sorry A spoke. A allays do wrong thing. But A did so 'ope as tha might coom. Tha sees A got used to moother. A got used to 'earin 'er cuss me. A got used to doin' for 'er an' A've nought to do in th' evenings now. It's terrible lonesome in' th' neeght-time. An' when notion coom to me, A thowt as A'd mention un to thee casual.

SARAH: Dost mean it, Sam Horrocks? Dost tha know what tha's sayin', or is tha foolin' me?

SAM: O' course A mean it. Tha sees A'm not a marryin' sort. Th' lasses won't look at me. A'm silly Sam to them, A knaws it. A've a slate loose, A shan't never get wed. A thowt A'd meebe a chance wi' yon lass as were 'ere wi' thee, but hoo towld me A were too late. A allays were slow. A left askin' too long an' A've missed 'er. A gets good money, Mrs Ormerod, but A canna talk to a young wench. They maks me go 'ot and cowld all over. An' when curate towld me as tha was to go to workus, A thowt A'd a chance wi' thee. A knaw'd it weren't a big chance, because my plaice ain't much cop after what tha's bin used to 'ere. A've got no fine fixin's nor big chairs an' things like as tha used to 'ave. Eh, but A would 'ave loved to do for thee as A used to do for ma moother, an' when A yeerd thee talkin' now an' callin' me a fool an' th' rest, by gum, A just yearned to 'ave thee for allays. Tha'd fill 'er plaice wunnerful well. A'd just a' loved to adopt thee.

SARAH: To adopt me?

SAM: Ay, for a moother. A'm sorry tha can't see thy way to let me. A didn't mean no offence. *(He turns to the door.)*

SARAH: 'Ere lad, tha tell me this. If A'd said tha might tak' me for thy moother, what wouldst ha' done?

SAM: Why kissed thee, an' takken thee oop in ma arms whoam to thy bed. It's standin' ready in yonder wi' clean sheets an' all, an' a new quilt from Co-op. A 'opes you'll pardon th' liberty o' mentioning it.

SARAH: A new quilt, Sam? What's colour?

SAM: Red, wi' blue stripes down 'er.

SARAH: A'm not a light weight, tha knows.

SAM: A'd carry thee easy – 'Strong in th' arm and weak in th' yead.' It's an ould sayin', but it's a good un, an' it fits.

SARAH: Wilt tha try, Sam Horrocks? God bless thee, wilt tha try, lad?

SAM: Dost mean it, Mrs Ormerod? Dost mean tha'll coom? Tha's not coddin' a feller, art tha?

SARAH: No, A'm not coddin'. Kiss me, Sam, my son.

He kisses her and lifts her in his arms.

SAM: By gum, but that were good. A'll coom back fur thy box.

SARAH: Carry me careful, tha great luny. A'm not a sack o' flour.

SAM: Eh, but A likes to year thee talk. Yon was real mootherly, it were.

SAM exits through the door carrying her, and the clink of the latch is heard as – the curtain falls.

WWW.OBERONBOOKS.COM

Follow us on www.twitter.com/@oberonbooks
& www.facebook.com/OberonBooksLondon